Franz Bette

紅 X 線
首飾

Red X Thread
– Jewellery

Der rote Faden
– Schmuck

目錄

邵雅曼 Yaman Shao 3
我們開始的地方
The project — where we start
Das Projekt — ein Anfang

Sabine Runde 7
紅 X 線：Franz Bette首飾
Red X Thread: Franz Bette Jewellery
Der rote Faden: Franz Bette Schmuck

Franz Joseph Bette 85
資歷
Curriculum Vitae
Vita

我們開始的地方

永添藝術項目起始於創造一個可供探索、沉澱思考的平台，鼓勵創作結合跨藝術、科技、技術等思想先進的領域，並關注於當代議題之上。今次，我們與德國法蘭克福應用藝術博物館合作“紅X線：Franz Bette首飾”特展，希望將其對於當代首飾的關注介紹到台灣，並討論關於它與社會之間的關係以及在藝術的定位。

永添藝術自許鼓勵正面的創作能量，指向更好的社會與永續性。海洋之於高雄、台灣，從歷史與文化的角度來看，始終是這個城市最重要的母體，轉化出這些圍繞著我們生活且具有變革性之力量。這項合作所代表的，不僅止於介紹當今藝術，更深一層的含意是希望去創造一種世界的連結；最重要的是，無分國界的溝通。

承繼兩檔重要大展：“Ornament without Ornament” 2007年於德國法蘭克福應用藝術博物館，以及“Same but Different” 2014年假國立臺灣博物館南門園區、國立台灣工藝研究發展中心主辦，永添藝術很榮幸能在此次展覽中介紹藝術家Franz Bette最新首飾創作系列的集成，他歷年無間斷的教育工作、慷慨無私的創作經驗分享，已為他奠定了在應用藝術學界崇高的聲望。

我們在此至誠感謝Franz Bette對於這項計畫的投入與信任、德國法蘭克福應用藝術博物館的策展人Dr. Sabine Runde，她和藝術家以逾兩年的時間與永添藝術合作討論、為此展覽注入新鮮的觀點與學術研究。我們感謝慷慨的借展單位德國哈瑙金工之家與佛茨海姆首飾博物館；這本美麗的書由法國巴黎Vier5團隊設計，德國攝影家Wolfgang Günzel攝影，Arnoldsche Art Publishers國際聯合出版，我們感謝他們的投入，更向執行英文編譯的Pamela Auburn，與中文編譯的Tracy Wang致上最深的謝意。Franz Bette在台灣的陶瓷實驗由台灣藝術家謝旻玲與顧上翎協助，對此，我由衷的感謝他們以及每一位團隊同仁的參與，驅使這項計畫得以轉動。

最後，特別感謝創辦人邵永添先生，他義無反顧的支持與信任，讓藝術家、藝術機構以及每一位創意工作者能全力伸展，這樣的項目將可以揭發我們平常可能忽視的盲點，並打開獨特觀看事情的角度，讓我們得以看見那些超乎期待之外，無盡的可能性。

邵雅曼
永添藝術執行長

The project — where we start

The ALIEN Art project began with the wish to create a platform of exploration, and reflection through encouraging the making of art and cross-disciplinary collaborations among artists, scientists, technicians and other leaders of thought who focus on contemporary issues. In this sense the exhibition titled "Red X Thread: Franz Bette Jewellery", in collaboration with the Museum Angewandte Kunst, Frankfurt am Main, Germany, draws attention to contemporary jewellery and contributes to the debate concerning the social relevance and place in art of this genre of decorative art which is quite new to Taiwan.

ALIEN Art sees itself as a mentor serving the sustainable development of a better society and regards the creative power of art and its positive energy as an important contribution to encourage this process.

Given the central role that the oceans have always had in the history and culture of Kaohsiung and Taiwan, ranging from being a point of transit to generating the all-pervading transformative energy which surrounds us, this collaboration represents more than just introducing the art of our time to the public; the deeper wish is to create a universal connection and, more importantly, universal communication.

Following the two major exhibitions "Ornament without Ornament" in 2007 at the Museum Angewandte Kunst Frankfurt am Main, Germany, and "Same but Different" in 2014 at National Taiwan Museum Nanmen Park, Taipei, held by NTCRI — ALIEN is delighted to show the latest works of Franz Bette, whose jewellery oeuvre, teaching activities and generosity of spirit have earned him high esteem in the field of applied art here.

ALIEN is greatly indebted to Franz Bette for his commitment to our project, which would not have come about with out his support. My deepest respect and gratitude go to the curator Dr Sabine Runde, Museum Angewandte Kunst, Frankfurt am Main, Germany, who developed the project with the artist and ALIEN over the last two years and combined fresh perspectives with scholarly research. We also thank our generous lenders, Deutsches Goldschmiedehaus Hanau, Germany, and the Schmuckmuseum Pforzheim, Germany, for their kind cooperation. This beautiful book was designed by Vier5, Paris, France; Wolfgang Günzel, Offenbach, Germany, took over the photography; publishing assistance is in the hands of Arnoldsche Art Publishers, Stuttgart, Germany. Our thanks go to them all. For the English translation and editing assistance, we thank Pamela Auburn. We are very obliged to Tracy Wang for the Chinese translation. Franz Bette found kind support from Min-Ling Hsieh and Shang-Ling Ku for their assistance in his porcelain experiment in Taiwan. In this respect I extend my thanks to each of them and every other single participant in facilitating the project.

Lastly our very special appreciation goes to the founder Yung-Tien Shao, for his support and unwavering trust in art practitioners, organisations and creative panels. Such projects can reveal blind spots we may seldom understand; to discover them opens new perspectives which make it possible to see beyond what has always been, to see beyond the limits.

Yaman Shao, Director, ALIEN Art, Kaohsiung, Taiwan

Das Projekt – ein Anfang

Das ALIEN Art Projekt startete mit dem Wunsch, durch interdisziplinäre Kollaborationen zwischen Künstlern, Wissenschaftlern, Technikern und anderen intellektuellen Wegbereitern einen Ort des Forschens und Reflektierens zu kreieren. In diesem Zusammenhang lenkt die Ausstellung „Der rote Faden: Franz Bette Schmuck“, die in Zusammenarbeit mit dem Museum Angewandte Kunst in Frankfurt am Main entstand, die Aufmerksamkeit auf *Schmuck* und versteht sich als Beitrag zur aktuellen Debatte der künstlerischen Dimension und gesellschaftlichen Relevanz dieses für Taiwan eher jungen Genres angewandter Kunst.

ALIEN Art Centre versteht sich als Mentor im Dienst der nachhaltigen Gestaltung einer besseren Gesellschaft und sieht in den schöpferischen Kräften der Kunst und ihrer positiven Energie einen wichtigen Baustein, diesen Prozess zu fördern.

Angesichts der zentralen Rolle, die der Ozean für Taiwan und Kaohsiung nicht nur geschichtlich und kulturell als geografische Gegebenheit und als Verbindung mit der Welt schon immer gehabt hat, sondern auch als durchdringende, transformative Energie, die uns umgibt, repräsentiert dieses Konzept der Kollaboration für uns mehr, als unserem Publikum die Kunst unserer Zeit vorzustellen. Unser tieferes Anliegen ist es, eine universelle Verbindung und, heute vielleicht noch viel wichtiger, eine universelle Kommunikation zu ermöglichen.

ALIEN freut sich, dass es gelungen ist, Franz Bette, dessen Œuvre, Lehrtätigkeit und geistige Freigiebigkeit große Hochachtung in Taiwan genießen, für eine Präsentation in Kaohsiung gewinnen zu können. Anknüpfend an zwei bedeutende Ausstellungen zum Werk von Franz Bette, im Museum Angewandte Kunst in Frankfurt am Main (2007)[1] und im National Taiwan Museum Nanmen Park, Taiwan (2014)[2], zeigt das ALIEN aktuelle Arbeiten des Künstlers.

ALIEN ist Franz Bette für sein Engagement, mit dem er das Projekt von Anbeginn verfolgt hat, zu großem Dank verpflichtet. Ohne seine Unterstützung wäre das Projekt nicht zustande gekommen. Mein Dank und großer Respekt gilt ebenso Dr. Sabine Runde, Museum Angewandte Kunst, die über die vergangenen zwei Jahre das Projekt mit dem Künstler und ALIEN entwickelt und frische Perspektiven mit wissenschaftlicher Forschung verbunden hat. Großzügige Unterstützung und Kooperation haben wir auch von den Leihgebern, dem Deutschen Goldschmiedehaus Hanau und dem Schmuckmuseum Pforzheim, erfahren. Das wunderschöne Katalogbuch wurde von Vier5, Paris, gestaltet, die Fotografie übernahm Wolfgang Günzel, Offenbach, und die verlegerische Betreuung liegt in den Händen von Arnoldsche Art Publishers, Stuttgart. Unser Dank gilt ihnen allen. Die Übersetzung der Texte ins Englische und die redaktionelle Betreuung lag in den Händen von Pamela Auburn. Die chinesische Übersetzung übernahm Tracy Wang. Für die Realisierung seiner Experimente mit Porzellan fand Franz Bette in Taiwan wichtige Unterstützung durch Min-Ling Hsieh und Shang-Ling Ku. Daher richtet sich unser tiefer Dank an jeden Einzelnen, der zum Gelingen dieses Projektes beigetragen hat.

Schließlich möchten wir gegenüber dem Gründer des ALIEN Art, Yung-Tien Shao, unsere besondere Wertschätzung zum Ausdruck bringen. Er unterstützte auch dieses Projekt mit seinem unerschütterlichen Vertrauen in den Künstler, die Organisatoren wie die kreativen Gremien. Solche Projekte sind zunächst blinde Flecken, die wir nur annähernd verstehen. Sie zu entdecken, eröffnet neue Perspektiven, die uns erlauben, über dass, was immer schon da war, hinaus zu sehen.

Yaman Shao, Direktorin, ALIEN Art, Kaohsiung, Taiwan

[1] Sabine Runde, Ornament ohne Ornament, Franz Bette – Schmuck, Frankfurt am Main 2007.

[2] Pamela Auburn, Same but Different, Nan-Tou 2014.

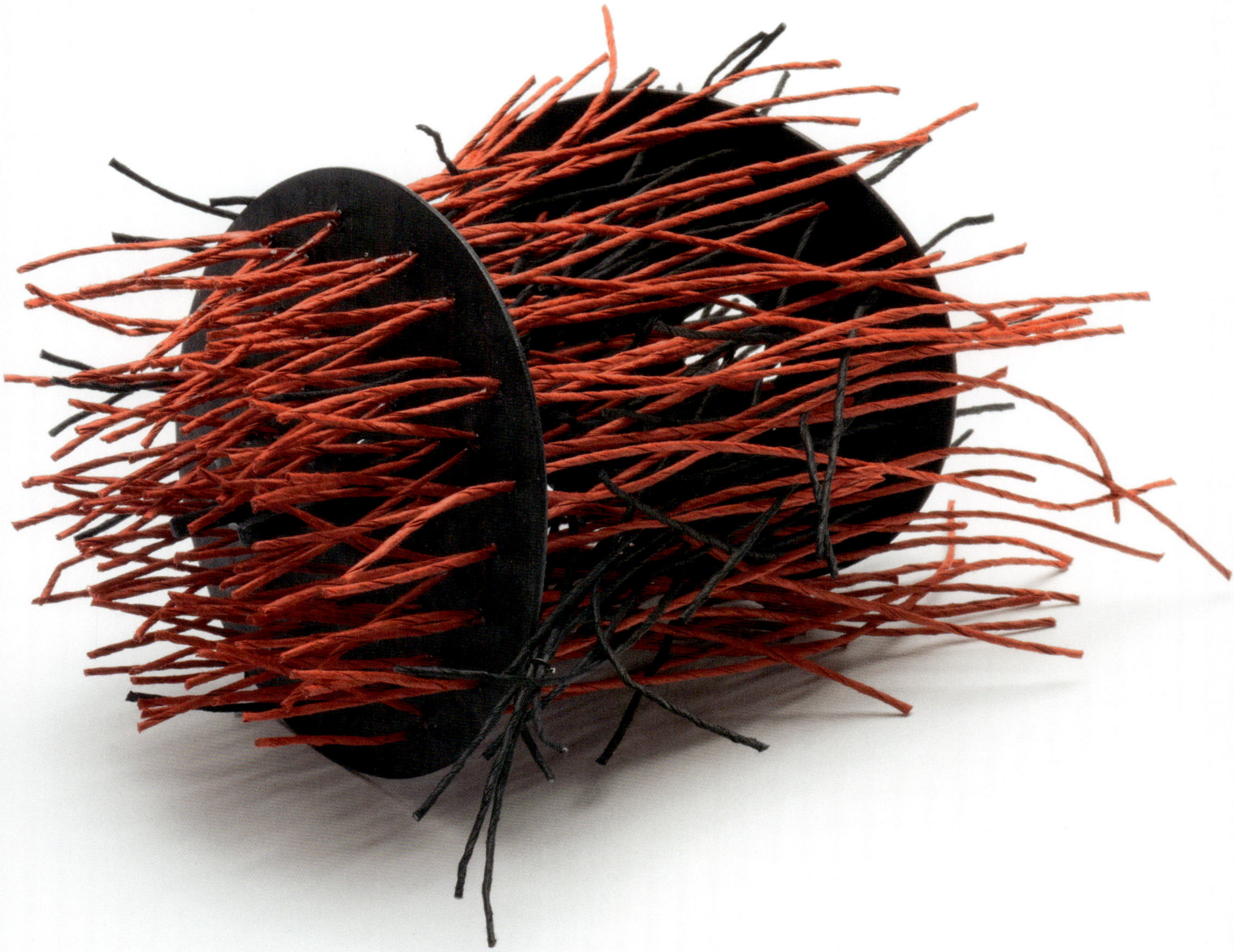

6

物件，木，顏料，紙繩

Object, wood, paint, paper cord

Objekt, Holz, Farbe, Papierschnur

2018, 14 x 11 x 9 cm

導言

首飾是藝術性表達的媒介，參照德文的意義為"創述首飾"，目前在亞洲引發了一股年輕的風潮。以當代的角度來詮釋首飾，多半錨重於西方思維。台灣高雄的永添藝術為本類型的現代藝術開展了一個平台，觸及更寬廣的領域，實屬世界面向的不凡創舉。

Introduction

Jewellery as a medium of artistic expression, referred to as author jewellery in Germany, has triggered a relatively new movement in Asia. The interpretation of *jewellery* from this contemporary perspective is primarily anchored in Western thought. In this respect the concept of ALIEN Art Centre in Kaohsiung, Taiwan, to open a platform for this genre of the modern arts as part of its broader agenda is a globally oriented, ambitious intention.

Einleitung

Schmuck als Medium des künstlerischen Ausdrucks, wofür in Deutschland der Begriff *Autorenschmuck* geprägt worden ist, löste im asiatischen Raum eine noch junge Bewegung aus. Die Interpretation von *Schmuck* aus dieser zeitgenössischen Perspektive ist maßgeblich im westlichen Denken verankert. Insofern ist das Konzept des ALIEN Art Centre in Kaohsiung, Taiwan, innerhalb seiner weit gefassten Planungen, eine Plattform für diese Gattung der Moderne zu eröffnen, ein global ausgerichtetes, ambitioniertes Vorhaben.

新面向的首飾發展在1960年開始於歐洲，篤信材質無價的思想意識風向球率先打破迷咒，把首飾從標榜傳統貴重金屬材質的價值裡解放出來。當代創述首飾的共識，是將材質與金錢價值分割，注重表達能力。同樣的，創述者的自我形象，不論是任何形式的本心隨意或是語有所指，都應該被解讀為藝術媒介 – 即為藝術最基本的條件。藝術的初衷對於作品的形狀或首飾強調的空間，有決定性的作用，例如物件外觀的形成或創造出來的感覺。而此藝術觀念的潛台詞則是與身體的關係 – 首飾穿戴者與個體物件的型式經由互動而浮出水面。

In Europe this new perspective of *jewellery* has been developing since the 1960s. In doing so the conceptual sphere already inherent in the non-utilitarian nature of the medium was first and foremost utilised to free *jewellery* from the constraints of valuable, so-called precious jewellery materials. In *author jewellery* today the consensus is to use materials independently of monetary value, which favour strength of expression. Equally one of the basic principles of the author's self-image is that form and freedom of intention as well as means of language should be understood as an artistic medium, a basic condition of art. The artistic intention is decisive for the form as well as for the space which *jewellery* addresses. Decisive to the way it is received is its appearance or the emotion it creates. A subtext of the artistic concept is the relationship to the body, which unfolds in interaction with the wearer and contributes independently of the format.

In Europa entwickelte sich diese neue Perspektive auf *Schmuck* seit den 1960er Jahren. Dabei wurde der gedankliche Raum, der bereits in der Zweckfreiheit des Mediums Schmuck angelegt ist, genutzt, den zeitgenössischen *Schmuck* zunächst von seiner in der westlichen Kultur verankerten Gebundenheit an wertvolle, sog. Schmuck-Materialien zu befreien. Heute ist es Konsens im *Autorenschmuck*, Werkstoffe unabhängig von ihrem materiellen Wert zugunsten ihrer Ausdruckskraft einzusetzen. Ebenso ist es eine wesentliche Grundlage des Selbstverständnisses der *Autoren*, Form und Freiheit der Sprachmittel sowie Intentionen als Medien der Kunst zu begreifen. Die künstlerische Intention ist bestimmend: für die Form und den Raum, den *Schmuck* bespielt. Bestimmend für die Rezeption sind das Bild oder die Emotion, die der Autor kreiert. Als Subtext, über dem sich die künstlerische Konzeption entfaltet, wirkt der Bezug zum Körper, der unabhängig vom Format des Werkes mitspricht und sich in der Interaktion mit dem Träger entfaltet.

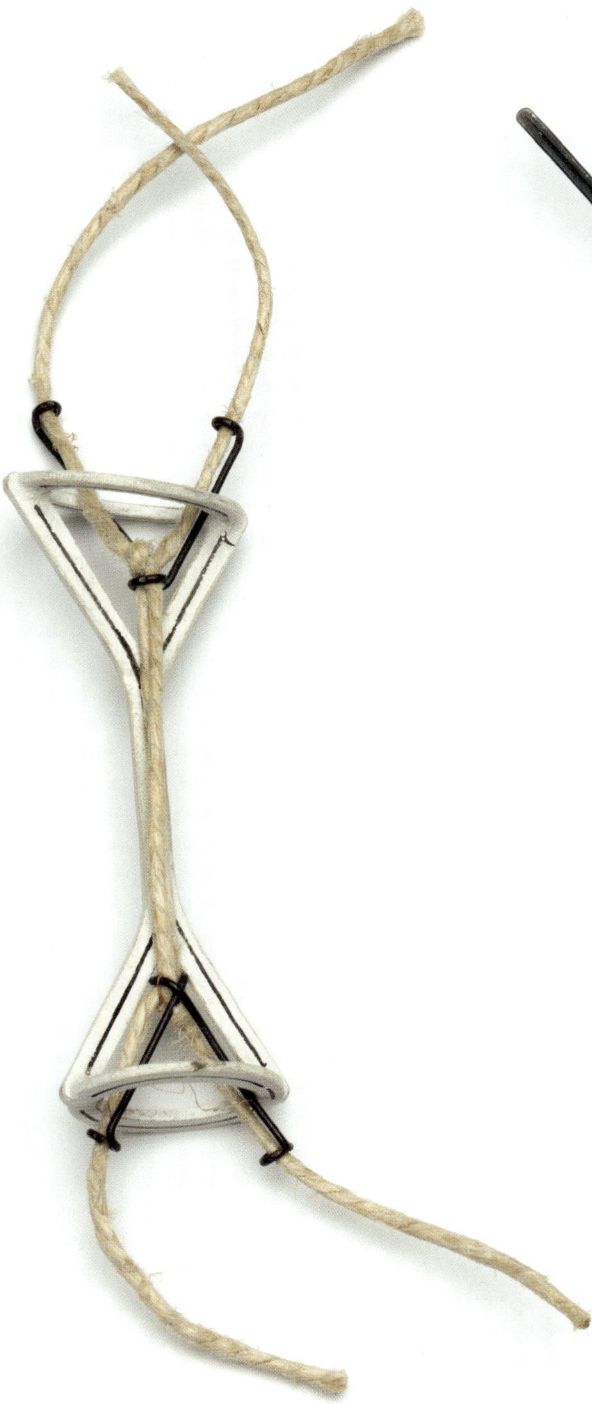

物件，合板，線材，低碳鋼絲
Object, plywood, string, mild steel wire
Objekt, Schichtholz, Schnur, Eisendraht
2010, 8 x 5 x 2.5 cm

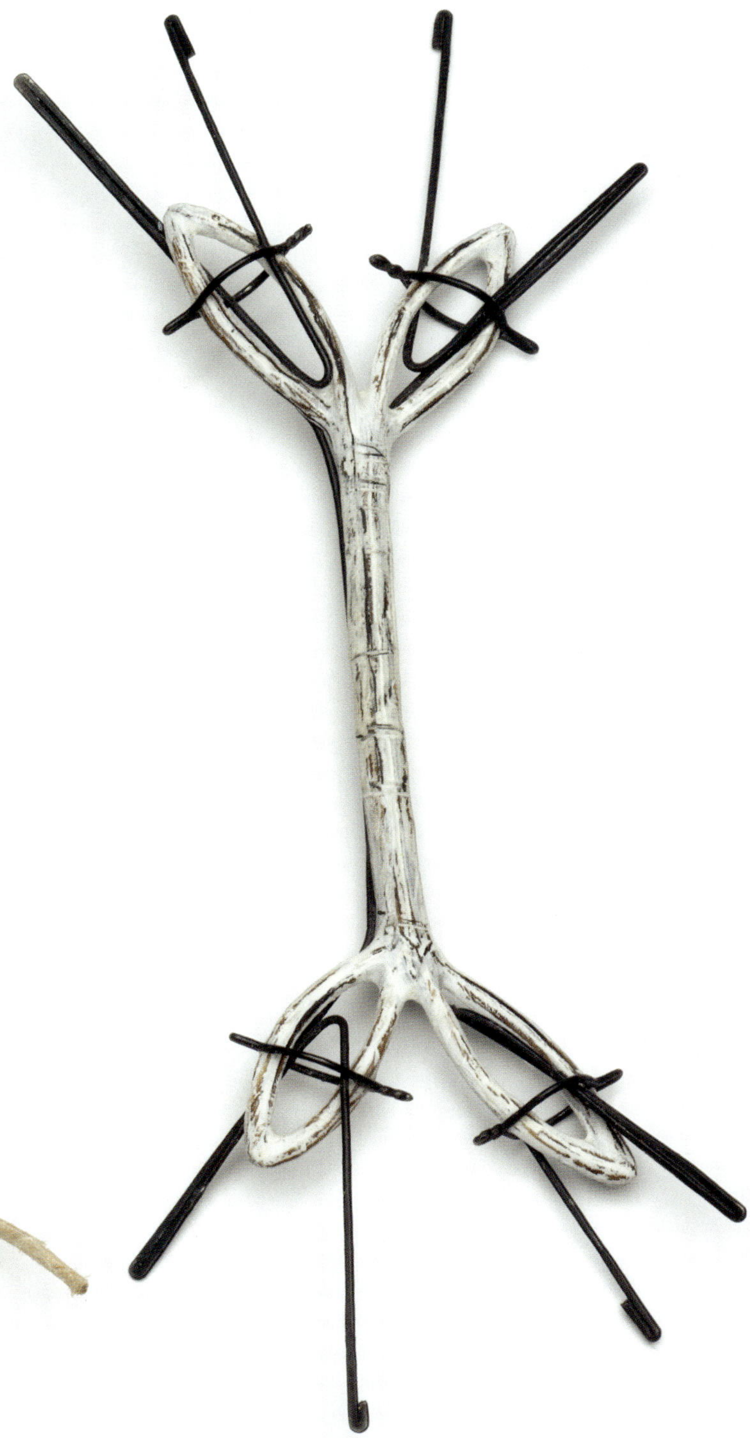

物件，花藝鐵絲，環氧樹脂，顏料，低碳鋼絲
Object, florist's wire, epoxy, paint, mild steel wire
Objekt, Blumendraht, Epoxidharz, Farbe, Eisendraht
2013, 10 x 4 x 2 cm

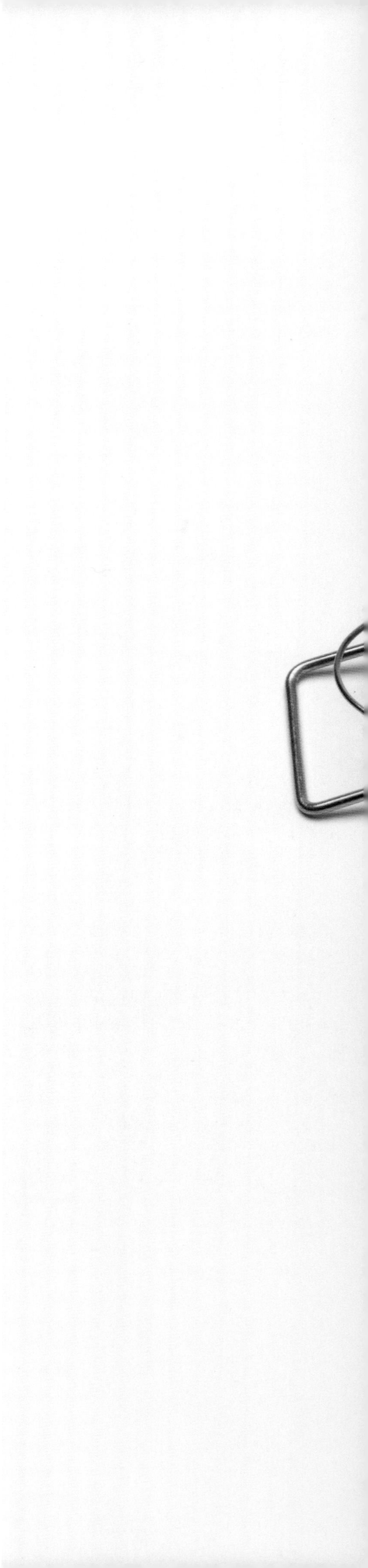

戒指,金,竹,不銹鋼,顏料
Ring, gold, bamboo, stainless steel, paint
Ring, Gold, Bambus, Edelstahl, Farbe
2008, 5 x 5 x 3 cm

戒指,不銹鋼,金
Ring, stainless steel, gold
Ring, Edelstahl, Gold
1983, 3 x 3 cm
Deutsches Goldschmiedehaus Hanau, Germany

戒指,合板,線材,低碳鋼絲
Ring, plywood, string, mild steel wire
Ring, Schichtholz, Schnur, Eisendraht
2010, 6 x 2.5 x 1 cm

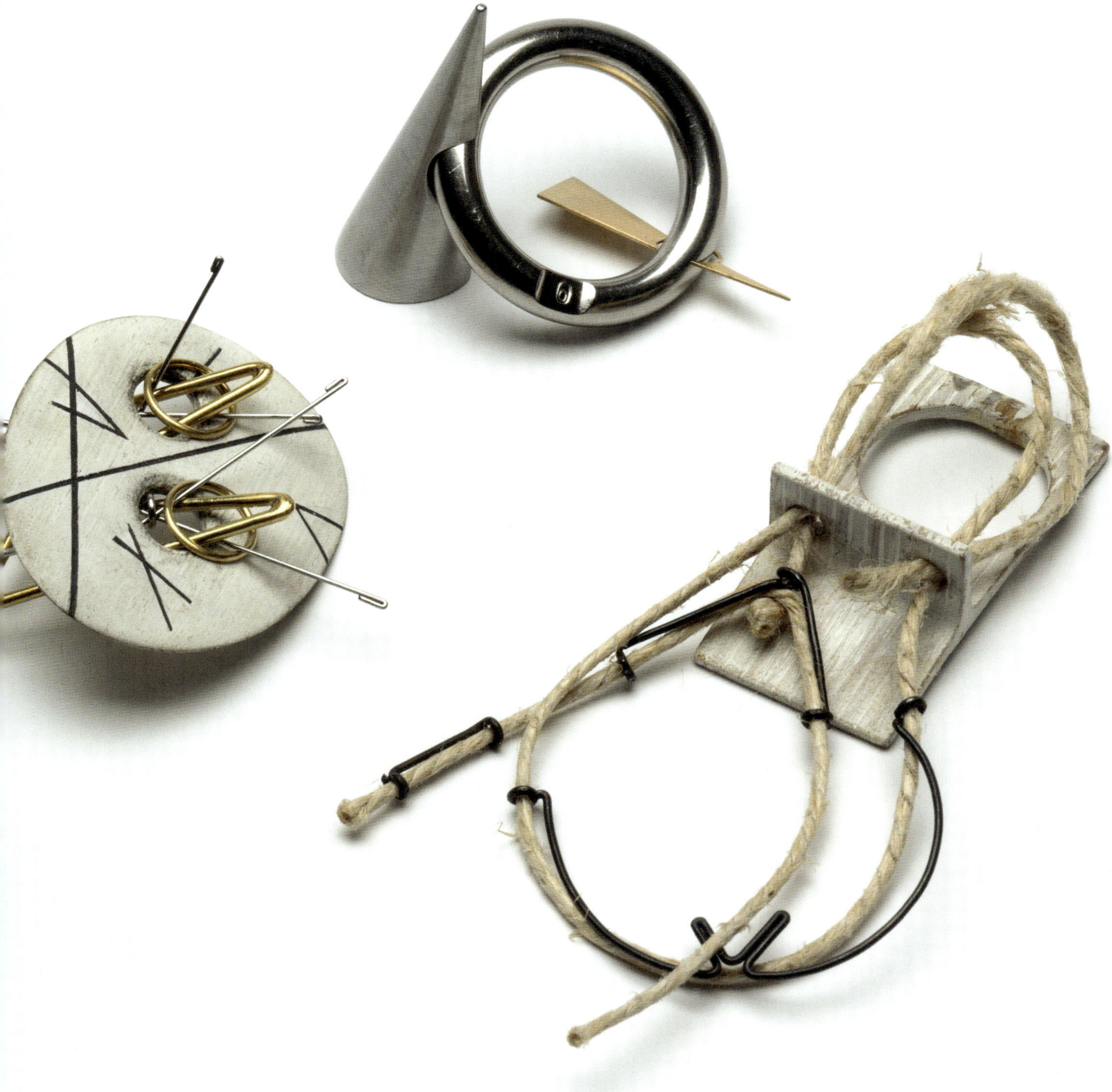

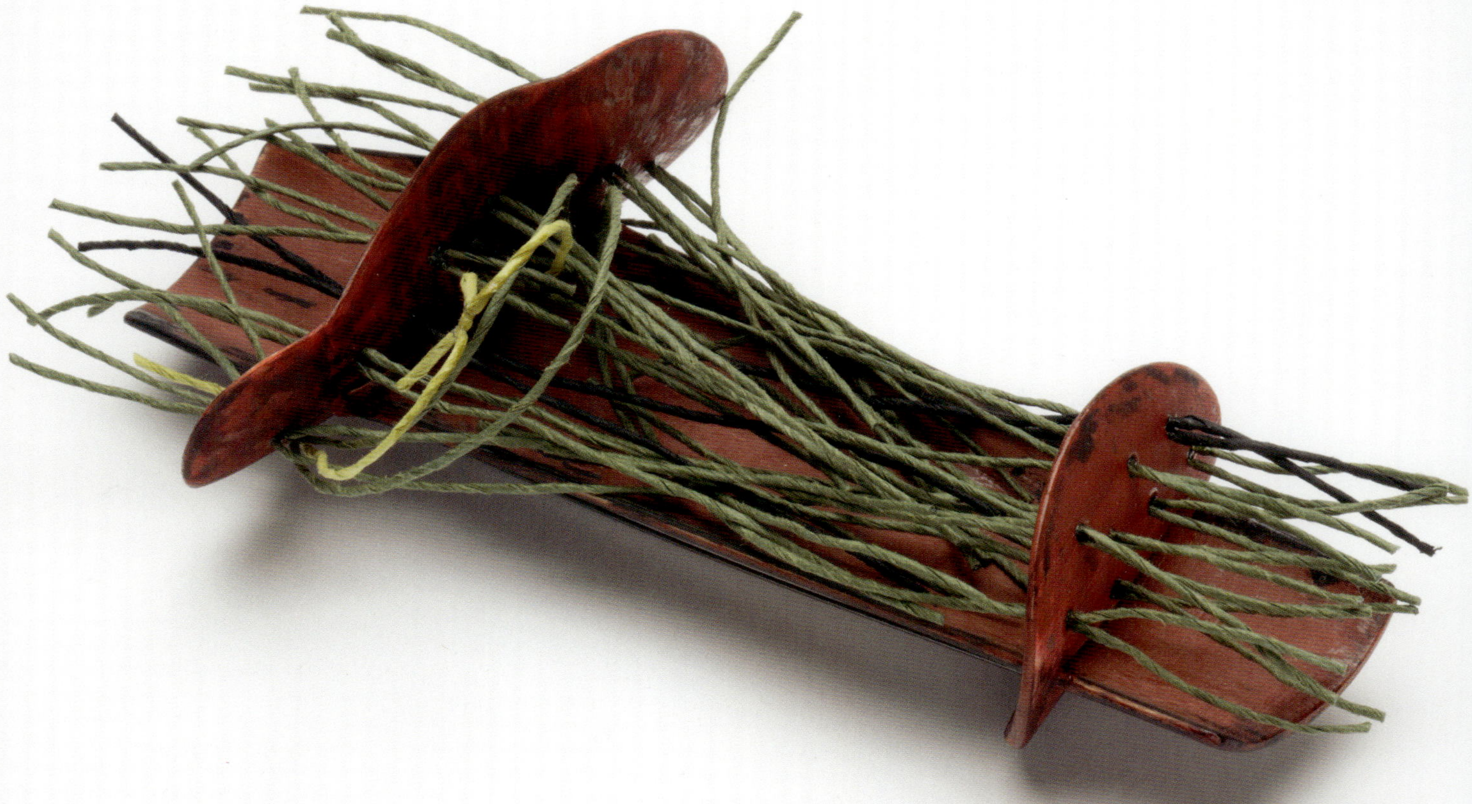

12 胸針,竹,顏料,紙繩
Brooch, bamboo, paint, paper cord
Brosche, Bambus, Farbe, Papierschnur
2018, 15 x 7 x 5 cm

法蘭茲·貝特對於設計議題探討與首飾構成的嚴謹辯證已有超過五十年的經驗，特別是概念性與創作生成的取法。直到今日，教學和永遠準備好要分享藝術創作過程的點滴與傳承，仍是他的工作之一。除了專注於本身的創作，傳達對於通俗設計、產品設計與首飾設計等範疇裡藝術化的可能性，更是對他十分重要。基於這樣的興趣與期望，世界各地的教學邀約更證明了對於他的能力之敬重，如愛爾蘭基爾肯尼、德國杜塞道夫和哈瑙、澳洲墨爾本和坎培拉、香港，以及近期的台灣台北和台南等地。

Franz Bette has been considering matters of design and critically examining the composition of *jewellery,* especially its conceptual and artistic formulation, for over 50 years. To this day, teaching and a great readiness to share his experience, disclose artistic processes and pass them on belong to his work. Apart from creating his own pieces, it is of great importance to him to convey artistic possibilities in the fields of general design, product design and *jewellery*. Because of this interest and expectation, teaching engagements such as Kilkenny, Ireland; Düsseldorf and Hanau, Germany; Melbourne and Canberra in Australia; Hong Kong, and more recently Taipei and Tainan, Taiwan, prove moreover the worldwide esteem for his abilities.

Franz Bette setzt sich seit über 50 Jahren grundsätzlich mit Gestaltung und insbesondere mit konzeptionellen und künstlerischen Fragestellungen zu *Schmuck* auseinander. Zu seinem Werk und seinen eigenen Arbeiten gehört bis heute immer die Lehrtätigkeit, verbunden mit einer großen Bereitschaft, seine Erfahrung zu teilen, künstlerische Prozesse offenzulegen und weiterzugeben. Das Vermitteln künstlerischer Möglichkeiten auf dem Gebiet der allgemeinen Gestaltung, des Designs und auf dem Gebiet *Schmuck* ist ihm ein tiefgehendes Anliegen. Aufgrund dieses Interesses und Anspruchs ziehen sich seit 1967 Lehrtätigkeiten durch sein Leben, die ihn nach Kilkenny in Irland, Düsseldorf und Hanau in Deutschland führten. Einladungen nach Bangkok in Thailand, Melbourne und Canberra in Australien, Hongkong und zuletzt mehrfach Taipeh und Tainan in Taiwan belegen zudem die weltweite Wertschätzung seiner Fähigkeiten.

在通訊發達的今日，世界各個角落似乎觸手可及，藝術也越來越國際化。而越是在這樣的時代，更是必須明智地按下暫停鍵，去注意藝術創造過程不可或缺的不同文化的根源，特別是察覺到思維過程的異同處。貝特在亞洲各地的教學，因融入而打開了許多在地經驗，這樣的多元性遠遠超越有距離感的全球觀！對於教學的熱忱，貝特擅長發掘出埋沒在不同文化裡的特殊天分，長時間濡染於此，方可觀其有物。

Today, when all parts of the world appear to be within easy reach through the possibilities of media communications, and art is considered to be so international, it seems appropriate to pause in order to give more attention to the different cultural roots from which artistic processes arise, especially to acknowledge the specific differences in thinking. Bette's teaching engagements in Asia have opened the way to a number of authentic experiences, which in their diversity go beyond the "global" encounter from afar. His interest in the students allowed him to discover the special talents inherent in their culture and, in doing so, time and time again to note how different the perspectives are.

Heute, da durch die medialen Kommunikationsmöglichkeiten alle Gegenden der Welt so greifbar nah wirken und sich die Kunst so international darstellt, scheint ein Innehalten angezeigt, um den unterschiedlichen kulturellen Wurzeln, aus denen künstlerische Prozesse erwachsen, mehr Aufmerksamkeit zu schenken, gerade auch aus Wertschätzung der spezifischen Unterschiede im Denken. Bettes Lehrtätigkeit in Asien hat ihm dazu eigene authentische Erfahrungen mit der dortigen Kultur eröffnet, die in ihrer Differenziertheit über die „globale" Begegnung aus der Ferne hinausgehen. Sein Interesse für die Studenten ließ ihn deren besondere, in ihrer Kultur verankerte Begabungen entdecken und dabei auch immer wieder wahrnehmen, wie verschieden sich die Sichtweisen zeigen.

手環，玉髓，金，祖母綠
Bracelet, chalcedony, gold, emerald
Armband, Calcedon, Gold, Smaragd
1973, 1.5 x 1.5 x 20 cm
Museum Angewandte Kunst, Frankfurt am Main, Germany

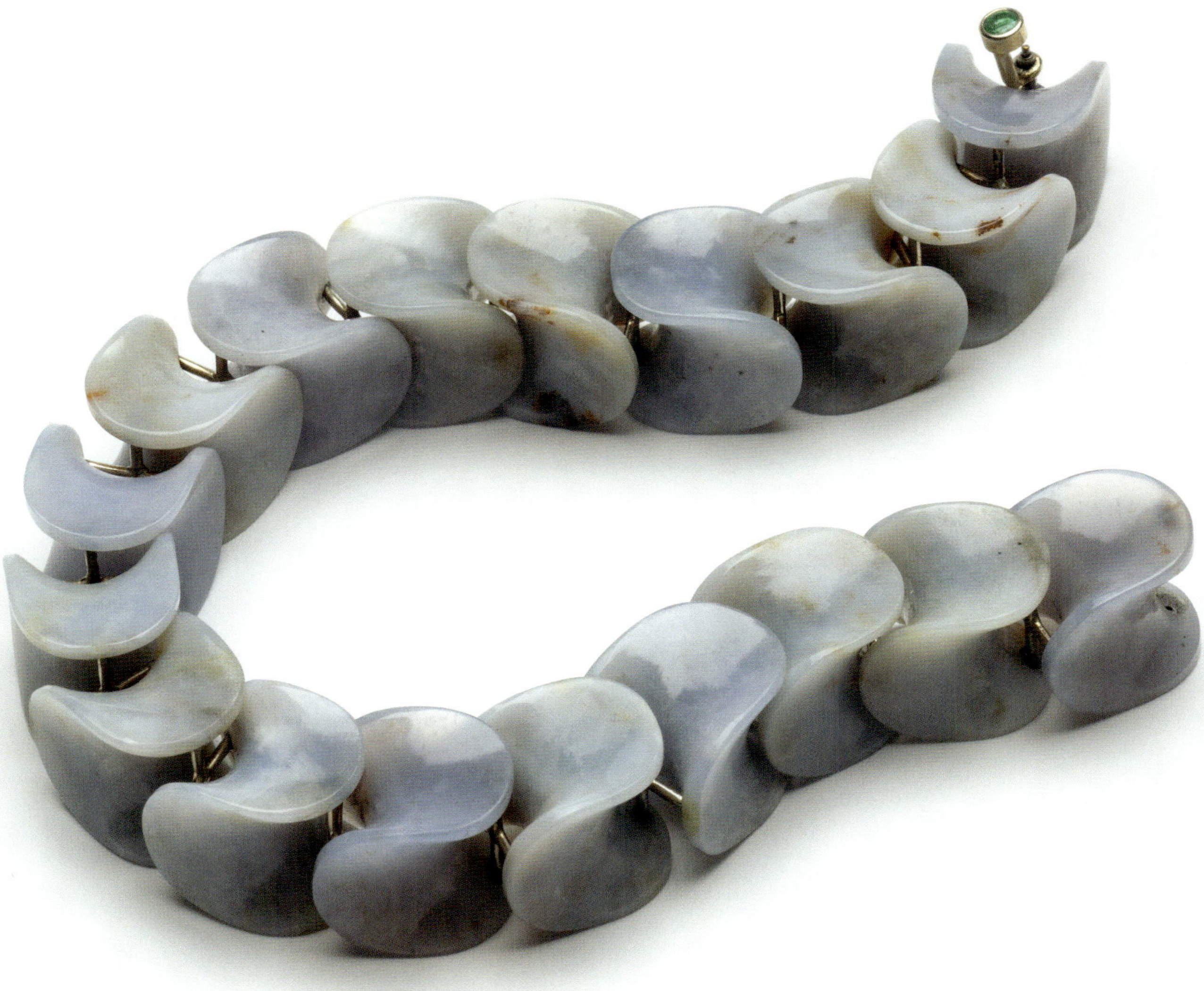

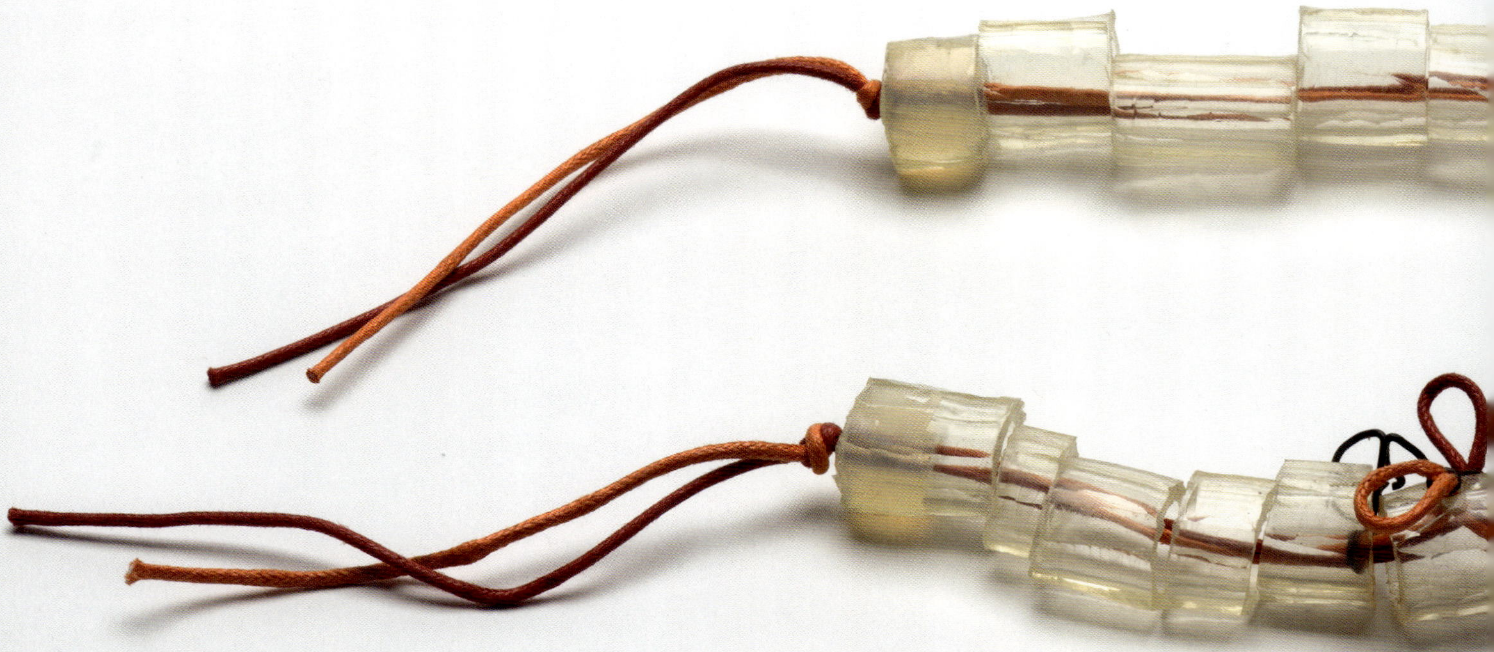

16 物件，塑膠元件，線繩，低碳鋼絲
Object, plastic elements, cord, mild steel wire
Objekt, Kunststoffelemente, Schnur, Eisendraht
2012, 24 x 2 cm

持續創作

法蘭茲·貝特生於德國中部，他的思路與創作有著歐陸文化的底蘊。為了本次在永添藝術·金馬賓館的展覽與在台灣的新觀眾，他內化在亞洲的親身經驗，發展了一整個系列的作品，也因此讓新的元素介入他的創作歷程中開出異卉。貝特在原先受西方影響下熟諳的金屬材質語彙，如鋼、銀或金 - 線狀、片狀或網狀；塑膠材質 – 用於表材或塑型，部份為事前灌色，部份為事後塗繪之外，增加了許多東方意涵的元素，例如瓷、紙、竹、木或編織等。在了解以上素材在傳統與亞洲文化的意義後，貝特更進一步地檢測與打磨，再憑著自身的創作目的與直覺發展出另一條道路。撇開傳統創作過程不論，他的文化影響、認知理解與各種感覺帶領著他跨步往前，不只在首飾界帶出新篇章，也更在探索特殊物件賦有的各種可能旨趣。

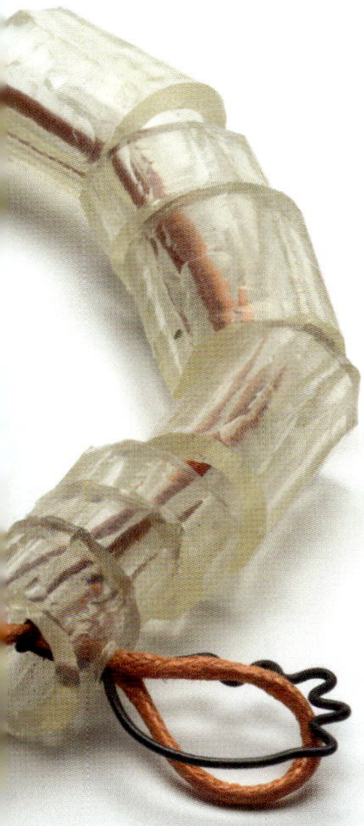

Work in Progress

Born in the middle of Germany, Franz Bette is a European artist; his thinking and his work are anchored in European culture.[1] For the exhibition in ALIEN Art Centre and for the new audience in Taiwan, he has developed a body of work which internalises his experiences in Asia. For this he allows new elements to intervene in his artistic approach. His Western-influenced vocabulary of metal – steel, silver or gold, in form of wire, sheet or mesh; and plastic, as surface or form, partly coloured, partly painted, has been expanded by materials with Asian connotations, such as porcelain, paper, bamboo, wood and textile. He works with these materials aware of the tradition and meaning anchored in the Asian culture; however, in examining and appropriating them, Franz Bette goes his own way according to his purpose or his intuition. Regardless of traditional working processes, his cultural influences, perceptions and feelings take the lead, bringing about a new repertoire orientated on jewellery but which also explores the possibilities of spacial objects.

[1] See Biographical Notes, in: S. Runde, Ornament without Ornament, Franz Bette Jewellery, Frankfurt am Main 2007, p. 118.

Prozessual

Geboren mitten in Deutschland ist Franz Bette ein europäischer Künstler, sein Denken und sein Schaffen sind in der europäischen Kunst und Kultur verankert.[1] Für die Ausstellung im ALIEN Art Centre und für das neue Publikum in Taiwan arbeitet er an einen Werkkomplex, der seine Erfahrungen in Asien internalisiert. Dafür lässt er neue Elemente in seine künstlerische Vorgehensweise intervenieren. Sein westlich geprägtes, materiales Vokabular aus Metall in Stahl, Silber oder Gold in Form von Draht, Flächen oder Sieben sowie Kunststoff als Fläche oder Körper, z.T. farbig, z.T. bemalt, erweitert er dafür durch asiatisch konnotierte Werkstoffe wie Porzellan, Papier, Bambus, Holz und textile Materialien. Mit diesen Materialien arbeitet er in dem Bewusstsein ihrer in der asiatischen Kultur verankerten Tradition und Bedeutung. In der Untersuchung und Aneignung dieser Materialien geht Franz Bette dagegen seinen eigenen Weg aus Planung und Intuition. Ungeachtet der traditionellen Verarbeitungstechniken lässt er, geleitet von seinen kulturellen Prägungen, seinen Wahrnehmungen und seinem Empfinden ein neues Repertoire entstehen, das er in den Dimensionen auf *Schmuck* ausrichtet, aber auch in seinen Möglichkeiten zum raum-greifenden Objekt hin exploriert.

[1] Siehe Biographisches, in: S. Runde, Franz Bette, Schmuck — Ornament ohne Ornament, Frankfurt am Main 2007, S. 119.

胸針,合板,顏料
Brooch, plywood, paint
Brosche, Schichtholz, Farbe
2012, 16 x 5 x 4 cm

戒指,不銹鋼,石榴石
Ring, stainless steel, garnet
Ring, Edelstahl, Granat
2002, 2 x 4 x 1 cm
Museum Angewandte Kunst, Frankfurt am Main, Germany

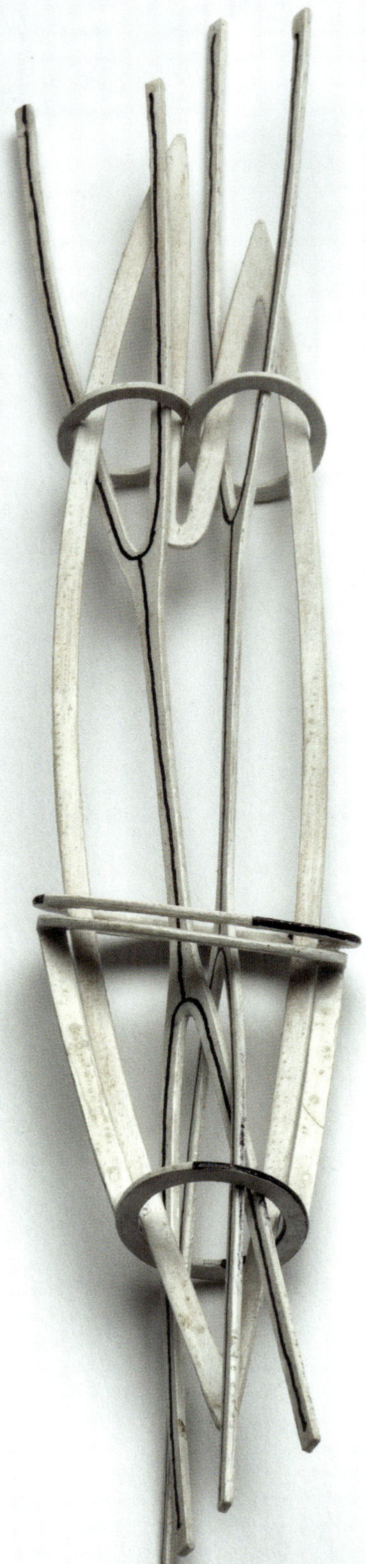

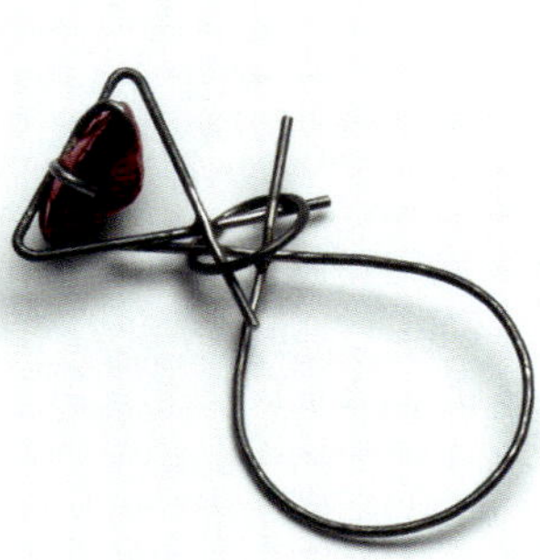

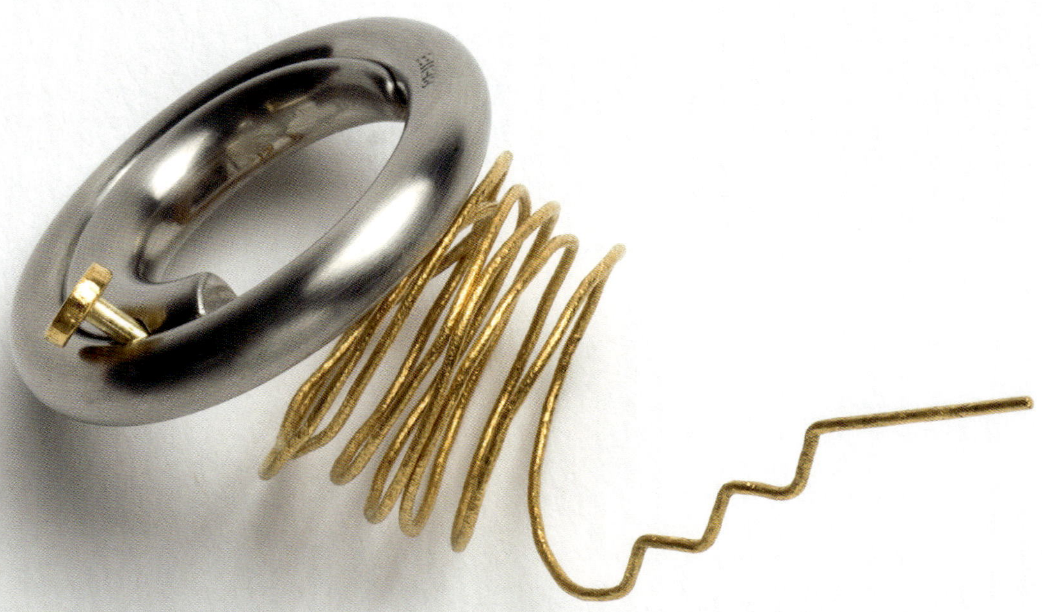

20

戒指，不鏽鋼，純金
Ring, stainless steel, fine gold
Ring, Edelstahl, Feingold
1983, 3 x 10 cm
Schmuckmuseum Pforzheim, Germany

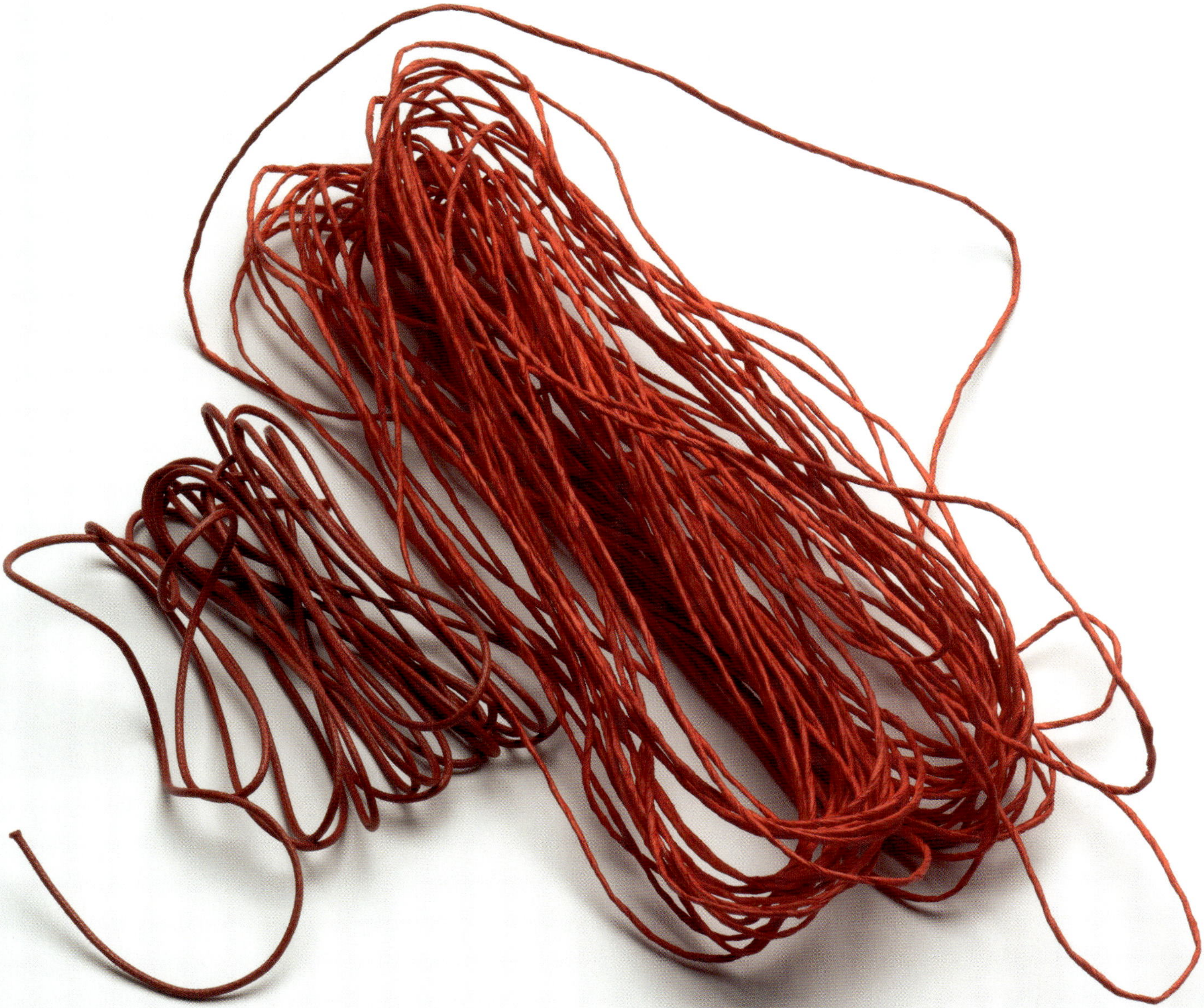

織品線繩，紙繩
Textile cord, paper cord
Texil- und Papierschnur

線繩

在本系列創作過程，主要元素慢慢結晶，如線般貫穿整系列的作品，捻絲成線絞線為繩，將所有材料集結綑綁。線繩，不若縫衣線薄弱，也不似麻繩粗實，是初生紡織抽出後織捻成紗，之後編紙為繩，貝特將此元素技術轉換為靈活自如的連結。

The Cord

During this process a central element crystallises which runs through this new complex of work like a common thread. As a medium it draws all the various materials together: it is the cord. Neither as thin as a sewing thread nor as thick as a rope, it is the first and foremost a type of cord made from spun fibres woven together and later a cord of paper. In a technical sense Bette puts this element to use as a flexible connector.

Die Schnur

In diesem Prozess kristallisiert sich ein zentrales Element heraus. Wie ein roter Faden zieht es sich durch diesen neuen Werkkomplex. Als Medium verschränkt es die unterschiedlichen Materialien untereinander: Es ist die Schnur. Nicht so dünn wie Nähgarn, auch nicht so dick wie ein Seil ist es zunächst eine Art Kordel, hergestellt aus miteinander verwobenen, aus Fasern gesponnenen Fäden, später eine Schnur aus Papier. Technisch gesehen wird dieses Element von Bette als flexible Verbindung konstruktiv eingesetzt.

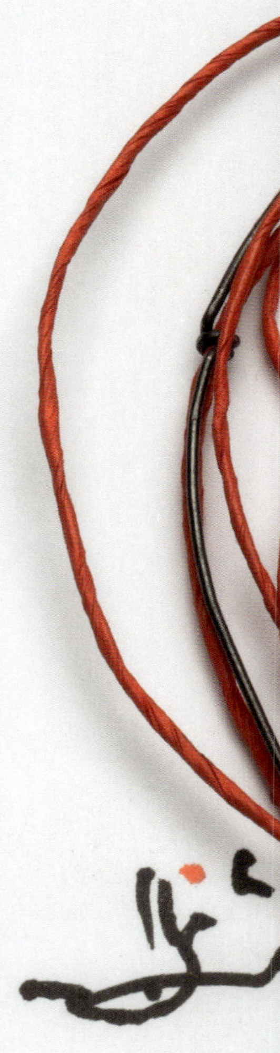

胸針，低碳鋼絲，紙繩
Brooch, mild steel wire, paper cord
Brosche, Eisendraht, Papierschnur
2018, 9 x 8 x 1 cm

草圖，紙，墨水
Sketch, paper, ink
Zeichnung, Papier, Tusche
2018, 14,8 x 21 cm

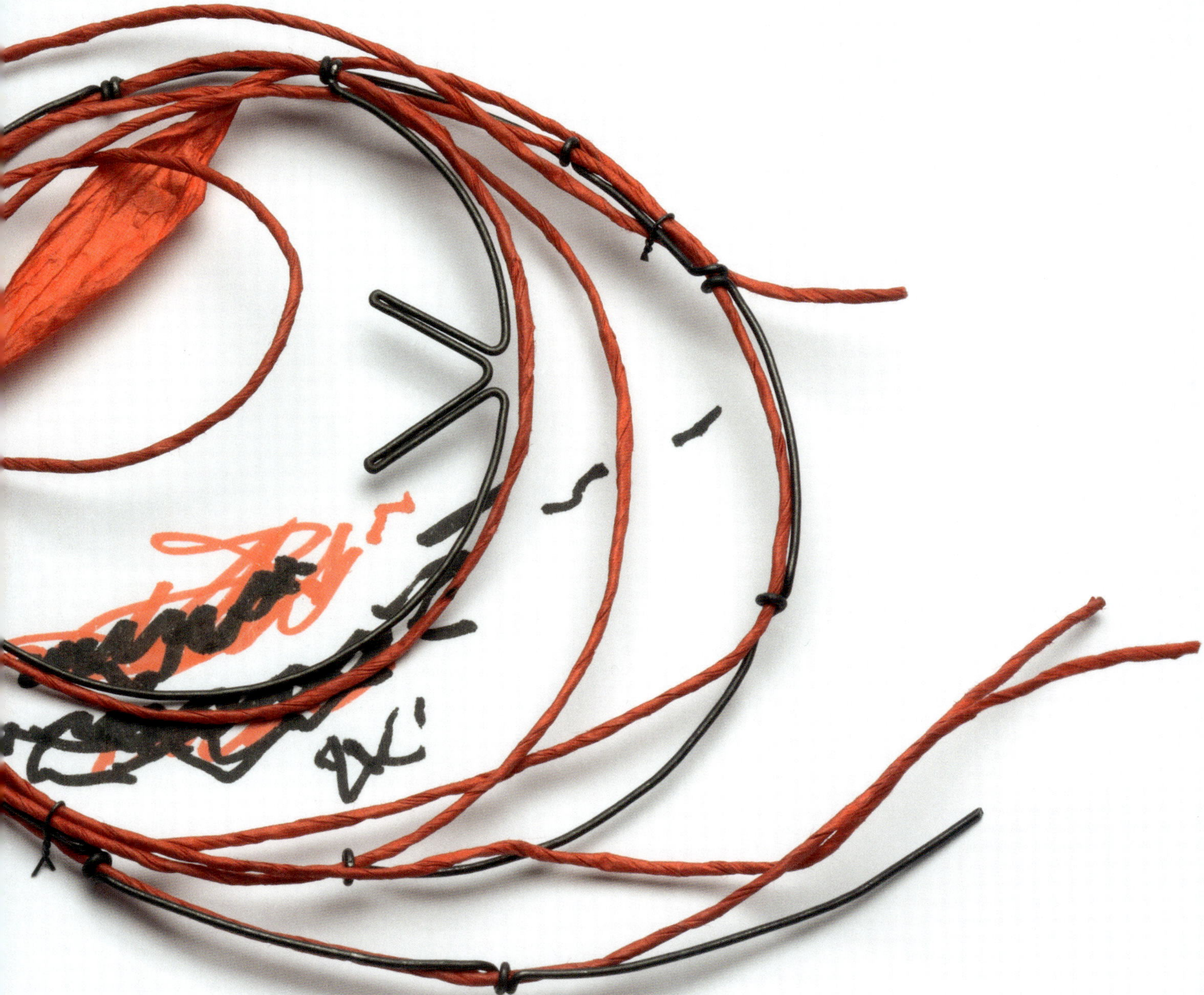

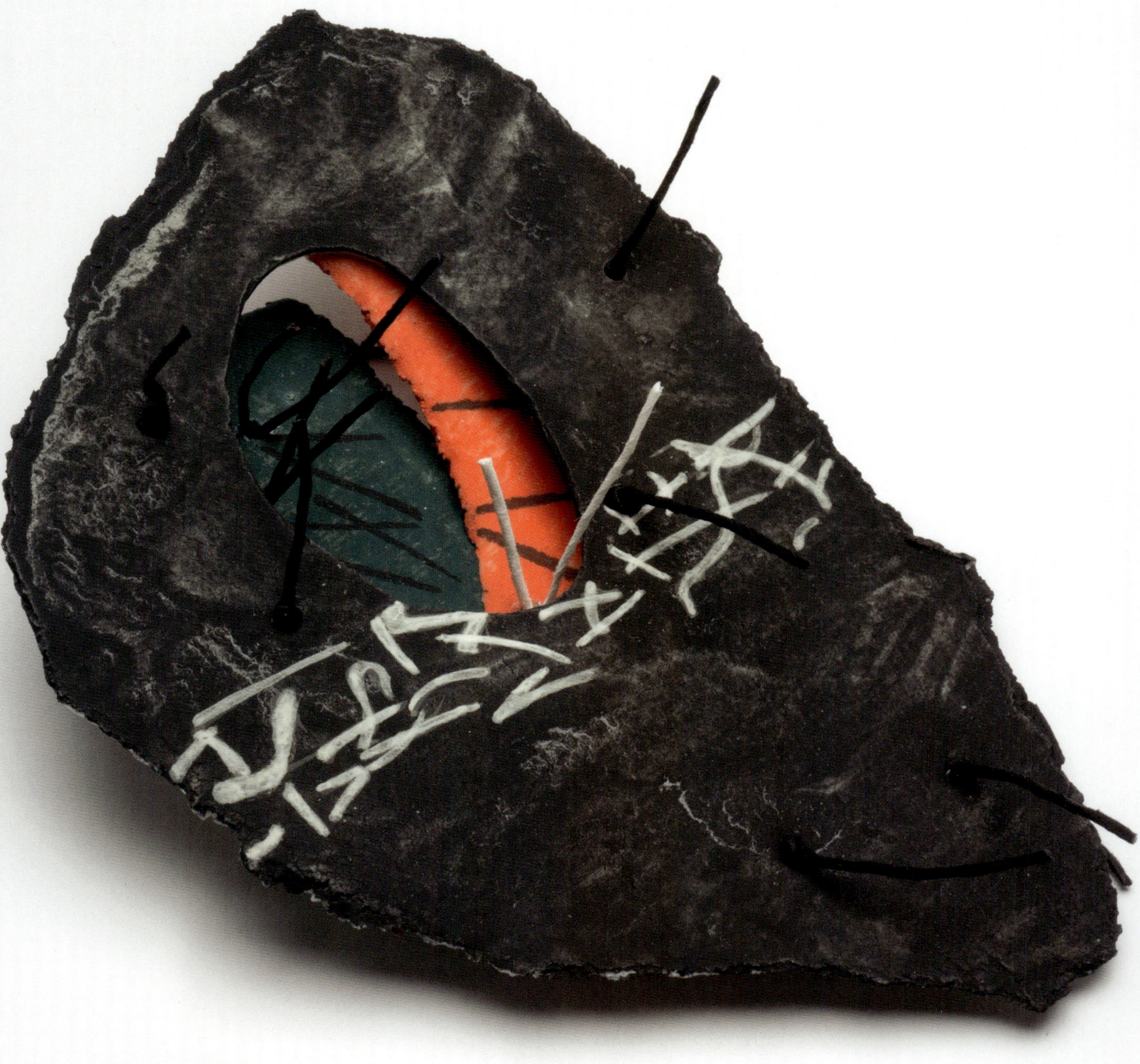

24

胸針，瓷，紙繩
Brooch, porcelain, paper cord
Brosche, Porzellan, Papierschnur
2018, 14 x 8 x 2 cm

法蘭茲·貝特依據此法持續發展,運用在他無懈可擊的工作方式與作品上,他創作的基本原則與核心主題,是將所有的元素靈動活潑地連結在一起。這個原則在作品的靈活機動與概念的移情上得到證實,尤如同本次展覽的文脈,在不同文化裡穿針引線。貝特創作的精髓是顯而易見的結構與動態,並總是能發現新的或更有趣的變化。以這樣的脈絡來走,對於早前創作階段的作品,其實是可以再次重新詮釋並深入探討發展。

In this way Franz Bette continues the process of developments, which applies to his unmistakeable working method and whole oeuvre. An elementary principle and central theme of his work is loosely connected elements. This principle has been proved in its flexibility and its conceptual transference, especially in the context of this exhibition project but also as a type of link between the cultures. The essential basis of Bette's creations is visibility of structure and movement, which are always realised in new, playful variations. Seen in this way, works from earlier creative phases can always be newly interpreted and further developed again and again.

Damit folgt Franz Bette seinen für sein gesamtes Œuvre geltenden und entwickelten, unverwechselbaren Vorgehensweisen. Ein elementares Prinzip und ein großes Thema seiner Arbeit ist die lose Verbindung der Elemente untereinander. Dieses Prinzip erweist sich in seiner Flexibilität und seinen gedanklichen Übertragungen gerade im Kontext dieses Ausstellungsprojektes auch als eine Art Link zwischen den Kulturen. Sichtbarkeit der Konstruktion und Bewegung, die Bette in immer neuen spielerischen Varianten realisiert, sind unverzichtbare Grundlage seiner Schöpfungen. So gesehen können Arbeiten aus früheren Schaffensphasen immer wieder neu interpretiert und weiterentwickelt werden.

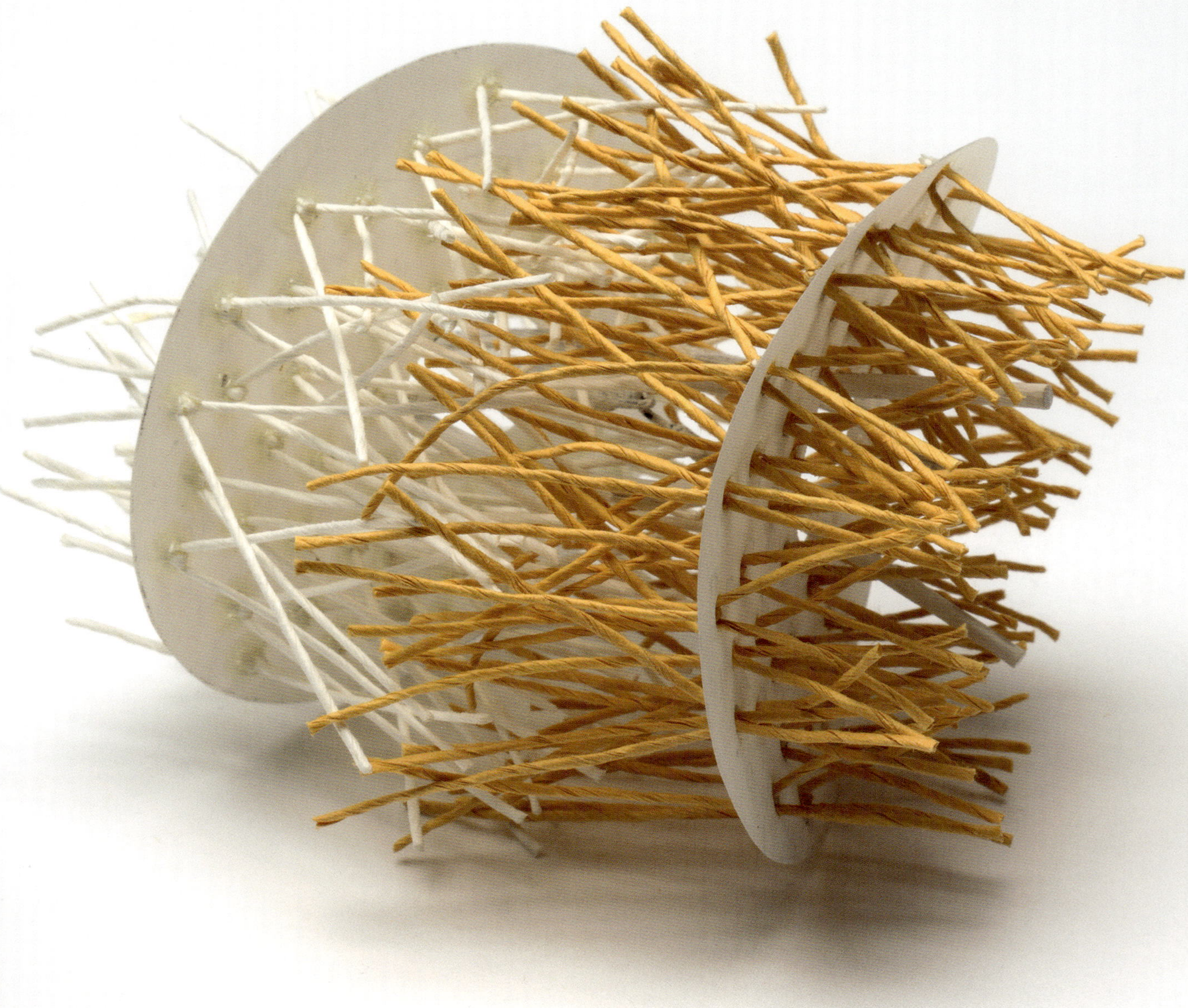

物件，厚描圖紙，紙繩
Object, transparent paper, paper cord
Objekt, Transparentpapier, Papierschnur
2018, 10 x 8 x 8 cm

在本次系列創作，線繩附加或取代貝特往常在構思概念所用的鋼絲元素。一開始選取這項素材的原因，是用創意的角度來觀察身脈導管，如擁有類似圖解形式的特質，以及在符號或翳影上有如手稿般的聯想；於是線繩成為了主角。先不論鋼絲與線繩兩樣物件在淺意識裡的較勁：硬與軟、光滑明確或是觸摸得到的組織質地，材質本身就是西方當代首飾非常具有爭議範圍的議題，同時也成為本次展覽的主題。本次主題固然觸碰到西方傳統感知的臨界，但對於藝術性表達的脈絡絕對是妥當正統。

然而亞洲的美食烹飪文化與西方飲食文化成對比，並不容許具有侵略性的表達，例如餐桌上不可放置個人刀具。這樣反映出來的，就是肉類通常是預先切好以便入口，而餐具的使用通常是筷子。有著尖刺的藩籬容易在這個文化裡越界，貝特清楚感知到兩種文化的差異，因此發現了連結的紐帶。

In this body of work, the cord appears in addition to or instead of steel wire, which in Franz Bette's conception is usually used as a constructive element. From the creative aspect this element appeals to Bette because of the ductus of the line, the potential of its graphic qualities and associations with script as symbol or as shadow. This role is taken over by the cord. Compared to the cord the fine steel wire conveys – apart from differences between hard and soft, clearly defined and textured – a subliminal aggression, a topic which has its place in the expressive scope of Western *contemporary jewellery* and has also been the subject of an exhibition.[2] In as much as this subject also touches limits in Western sensibilities, it is nevertheless legitimate in the context of an artistic intention.

However, in Asian culture aggressive expression is banned from its gastronomy, and in contrast to Western dining culture, one's personal knife is not allowed at the table. As a consequence, meat is served cut into bite-sized pieces, and chopsticks are used as eating tools. In this culture the spiked end of the wire crosses the boundary of sensibilities. Within these opposites of awareness, which describe cultural difference, Franz Bette discovers the cord.

[2] Arsenale – Aggression im Schmuck, ed. Forum für Schmuck und Design, exh. cat. Museum für Kunsthandwerk Frankfurt am Main / Deutsches Klingenmuseum Solingen, Cologne 1991.

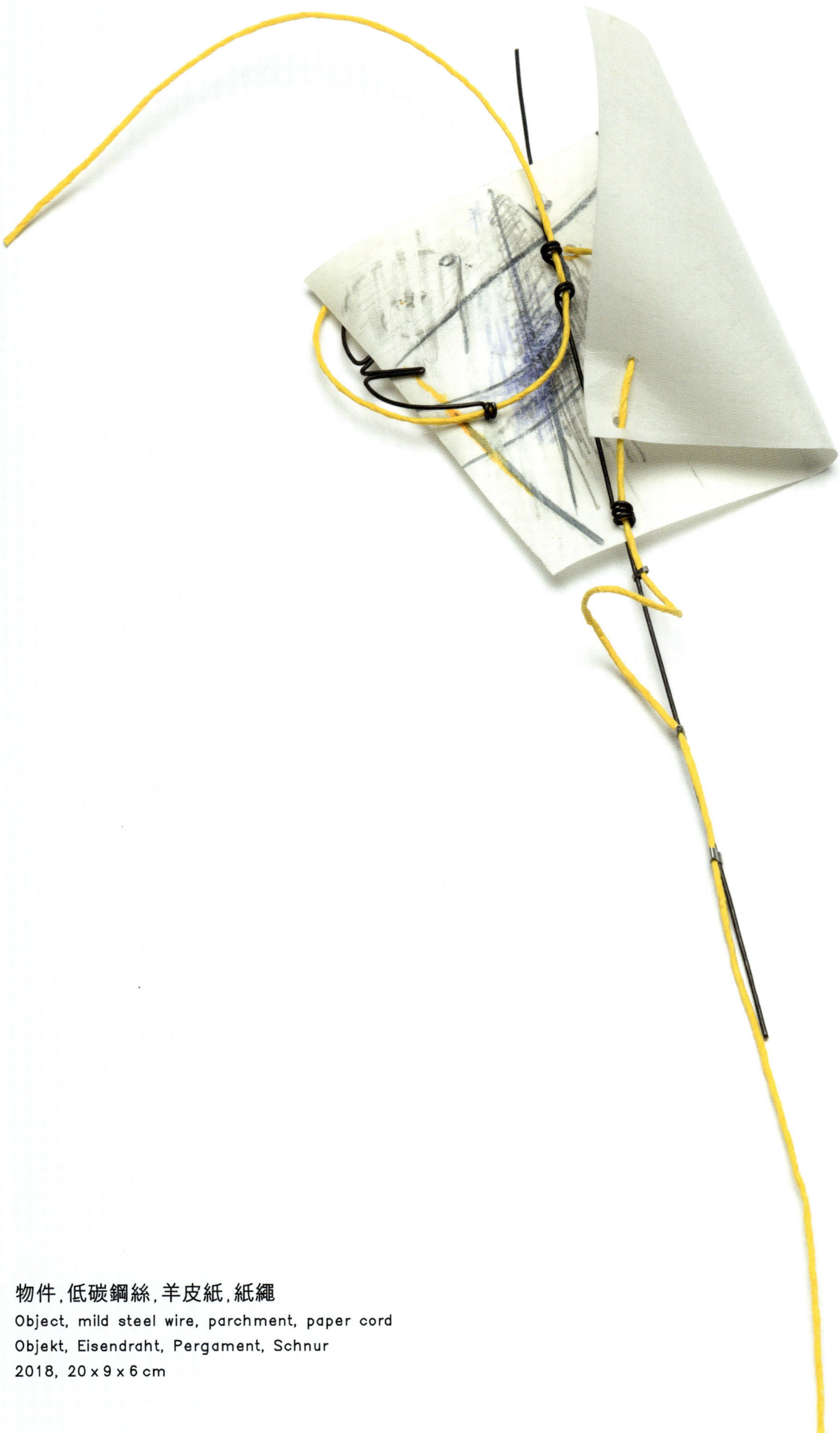

物件, 低碳鋼絲, 羊皮紙, 紙繩
Object, mild steel wire, parchment, paper cord
Objekt, Eisendraht, Pergament, Schnur
2018, 20 x 9 x 6 cm

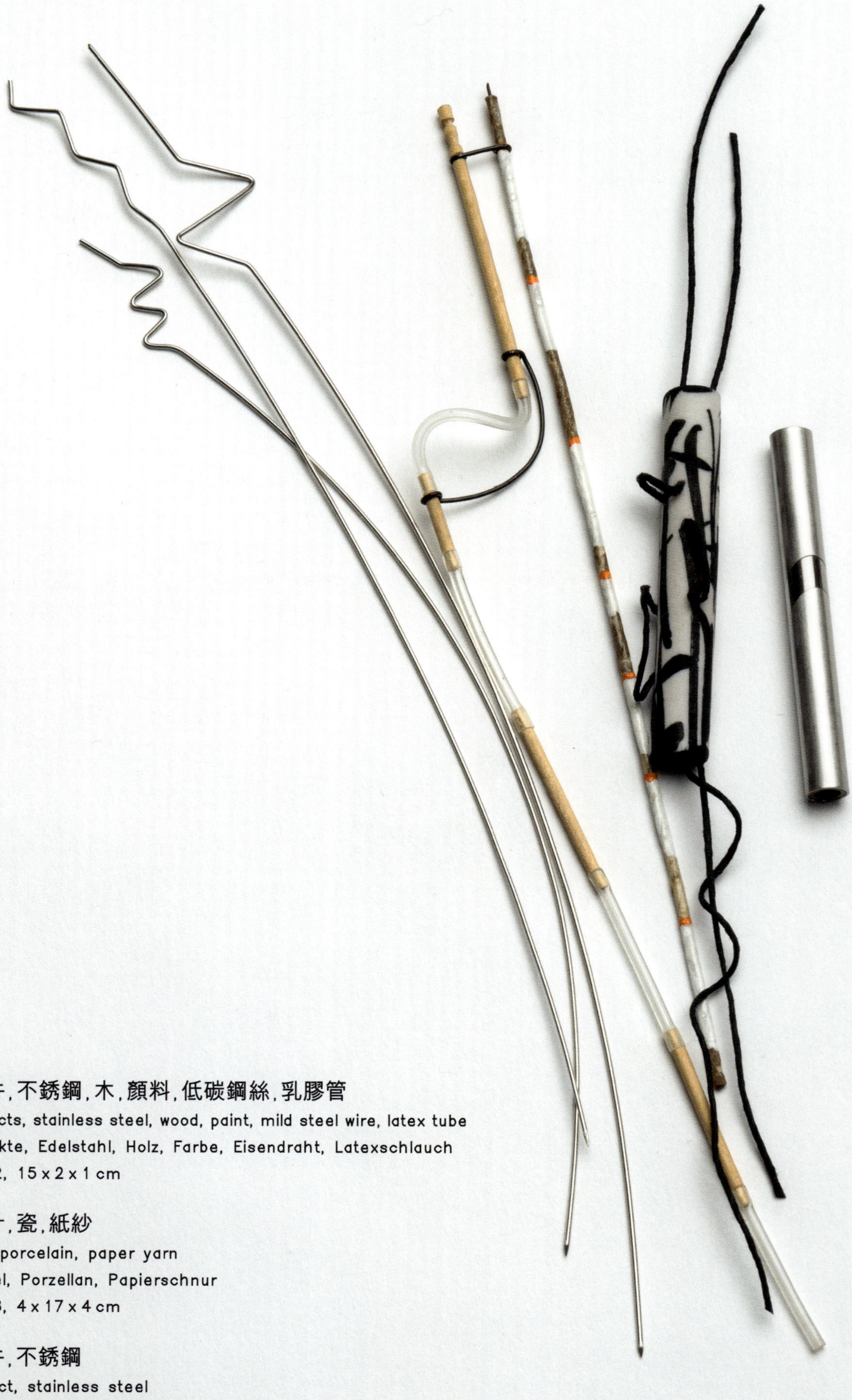

物件，不銹鋼，木，顏料，低碳鋼絲，乳膠管
Objects, stainless steel, wood, paint, mild steel wire, latex tube
Objekte, Edelstahl, Holz, Farbe, Eisendraht, Latexschlauch
2012, 15 x 2 x 1 cm

別針，瓷，紙紗
Pin, porcelain, paper yarn
Nadel, Porzellan, Papierschnur
2018, 4 x 17 x 4 cm

物件，不銹鋼
Object, stainless steel
Objekt, Edelstahl
1987, 8 x 0.8 cm

In diesem Werkkomplex tritt nun die Schnur neben oder an die Stelle von Stahldraht, den Franz Bette in seiner Konzeption sonst konstruktiv einsetzt. Gestalterisch reizt Bette bei diesem Element der Duktus der Linie, die Linie mit dem Potenzial zur Zeichnung, der Verbindung zur Schrift, als Zeichen oder Schatten. Diesen Part übernimmt jetzt die Schnur. Im Vergleich zur Schnur übermittelt der feine Stahldraht – über die Unterschiede zwischen weich und hart, strukturiert und klar definiert hinaus – trotz seiner Zartheit durch seine offenstehenden Enden eine unterschwellige Aggressivität, die in der westlichen *Schmuck-Moderne* zum Ausdrucksspektrum gehören kann und auch schon in eigenen Ausstellungen thematisiert worden ist.[2] Insofern berührt dieser Ausdruck auch im westlichen Empfinden eine Grenze, die jedoch im Kontext künstlerischer Intention legitimiert ist.

In der asiatischen Kultur jedoch, in der der Ausdruck der Aggression aus der Esskultur verbannt ist, eine Kultur, die – im Kontrast zur westlichen Tischkultur – das persönliche Messer am Tisch nicht zulässt, das Fleisch deshalb in Biss-großen Stücken serviert und Stäbchen als Esswerkzeug einsetzt, in dieser Kultur überschreitet der spitz auslaufende Draht in seinem Ausdruck eine Grenze im Empfinden. In dieser Gegensätzlichkeit der Wahrnehmung, die eine kulturelle Differenz beschreibt, entdeckt Franz Bette die Schnur.

[2] Arsenale – Aggression im Schmuck, hrsg. Forum für Schmuck und Design, Museum für Kunsthandwerk Frankfurt am Main / Deutsches Klingenmuseum Solingen, Köln 1991.

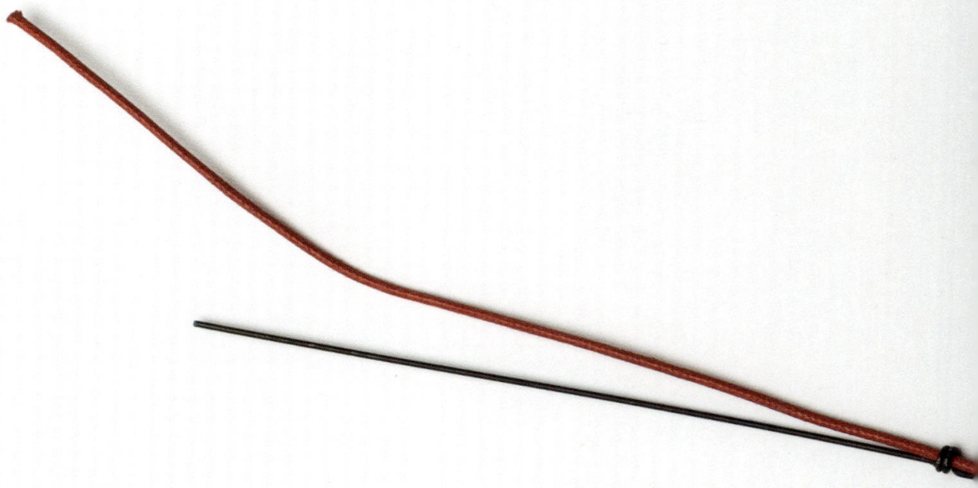

32

物件，低碳鋼絲，線繩
Object, mild steel wire, cord
Objekt, Eisendraht, Schnur
2012, 22 x 6 x 1 cm

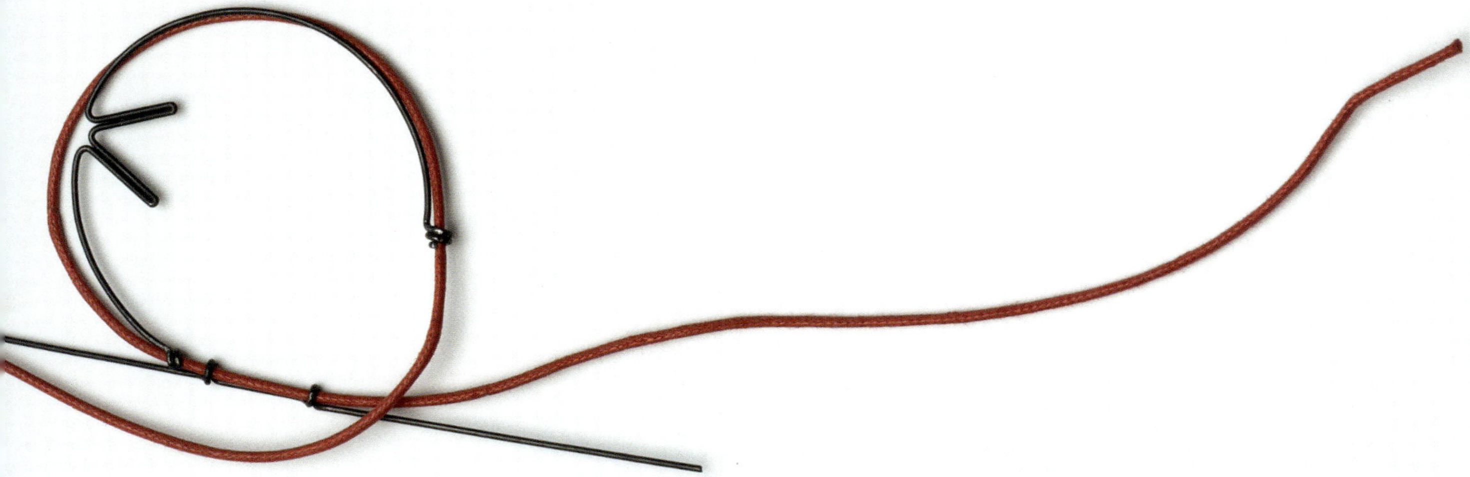

照著這樣的模式，對於他採用中國文化裡含有特殊意涵的繩結來創作，似乎就不只是偶發事件了。中式繩結早已運用於文人社會，不同於西方世界將貴重物如玉或其他寶石，鑲嵌在金屬或鍊成首飾；古人以絲繩結之，並將其當作首飾或幸運符來配戴。紅色彰顯幸運，根據中國五行的說法，將所有事件與元素在宇宙天地中各順其位安然共存，是謂吉。在今日，紅線繩在節慶與日常生中仍佔有一席之地。

In doing so he seemingly coincidentally picks up on an old tradition deeply anchored in Chinese culture, which ascribes special meaning to the cord. As an art form associated with extravagantly tied knots and bows, which could transport good luck messages, the cord was an element of jewellery for courtly society. Valuable things such as jade or other stones, which would be set in metal or worn on a chain as jewellery in the Western world, were tied on a cord and held by fanciful knots to be worn as jewellery or amulets in the Asian region. The luck-bringing attributes were intensified by the colour red, which according to the Chinese Five Elements teaching brings luck by setting all things and elements in the cosmos into relationship. Even today the use of a red cord continues during festivals and daily life.

Dabei knüpft er scheinbar zufällig an eine alte, tief in der chinesischen Kultur verwurzelte Tradition an, die der Schnur spezielle Bedeutung zumisst. In Verbindung mit aufwendig geknüpften Knoten und Schleifen, die glücksbringende Botschaften übermitteln können, war die Schnur als Kunstform Bestandteil des Schmucks auch der höfischen Gesellschaft. Kostbare Dinge, Jade oder andere Steine, die in der westlichen Welt in Metall gefasst oder an einer Kette als Schmuck getragen werden, knüpft man im asiatischen Raum an eine Schnur und trägt sie gehalten von phantasievollen Knoten als Schmuck oder Amulett. Verstärkt wird die glücksbringende Bedeutung durch die Farbe Rot, die innerhalb der chinesischen Fünf-Elemente-Lehre, die alle Dinge der Welt und des Kosmos zueinander in Beziehung setzt, eine glücksbringende Farbe ist. Noch heute zieht sich ihre Verwendung in Form der roten Schnur durch Festtage und Alltag.

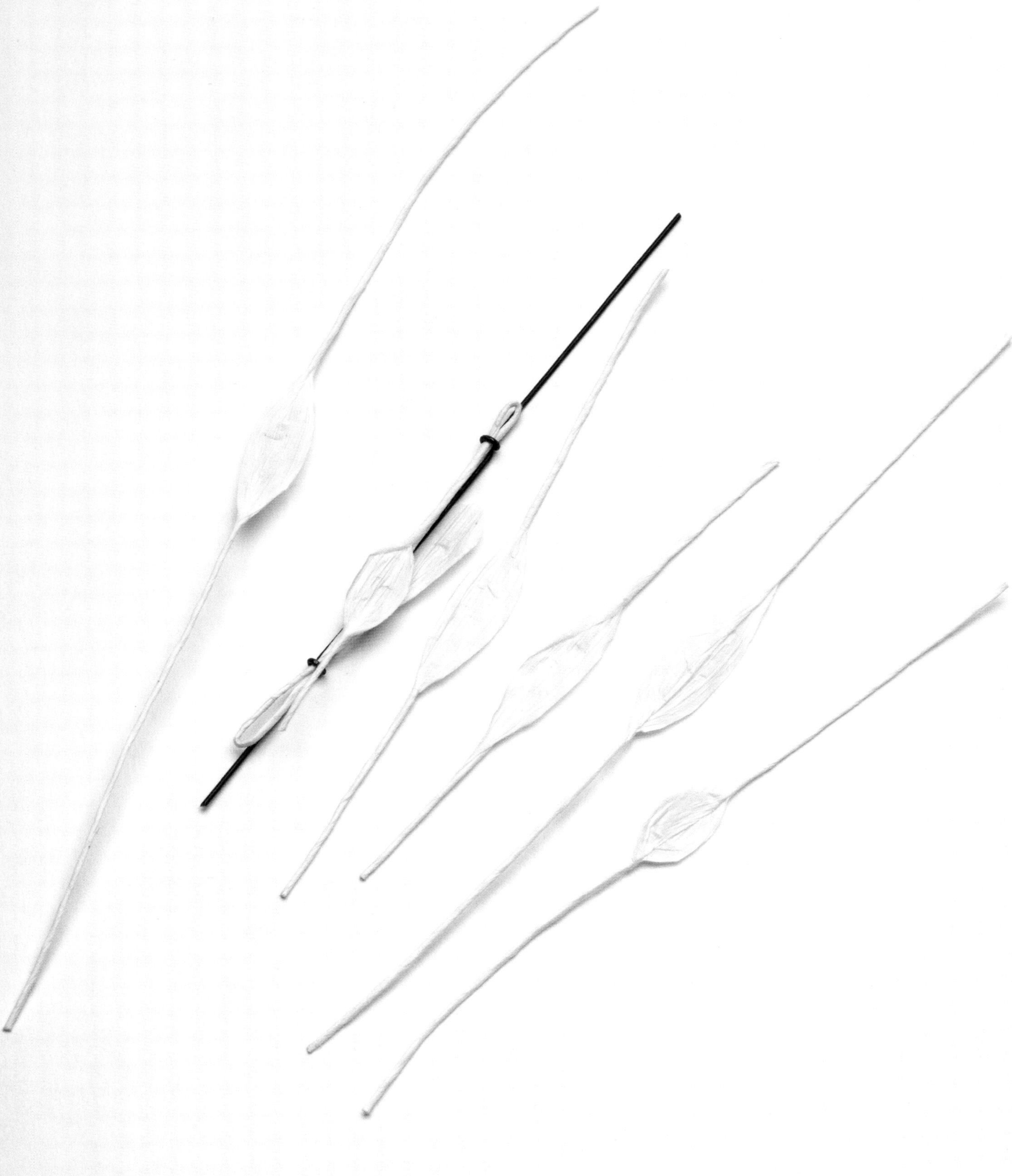

習作, 紙繩, 低碳鋼絲
Studies, paper cord, mild steel wire
Studien, Papierschnur, Eisendraht
2018, 10 – 15 cm

36

胸針，木，顏料，墨水，紙繩

Brooch, wood, paint, ink, paper cord

Brosche, Holz, Farbe, Papierschnur

2018, 10 x 12 x 4 cm

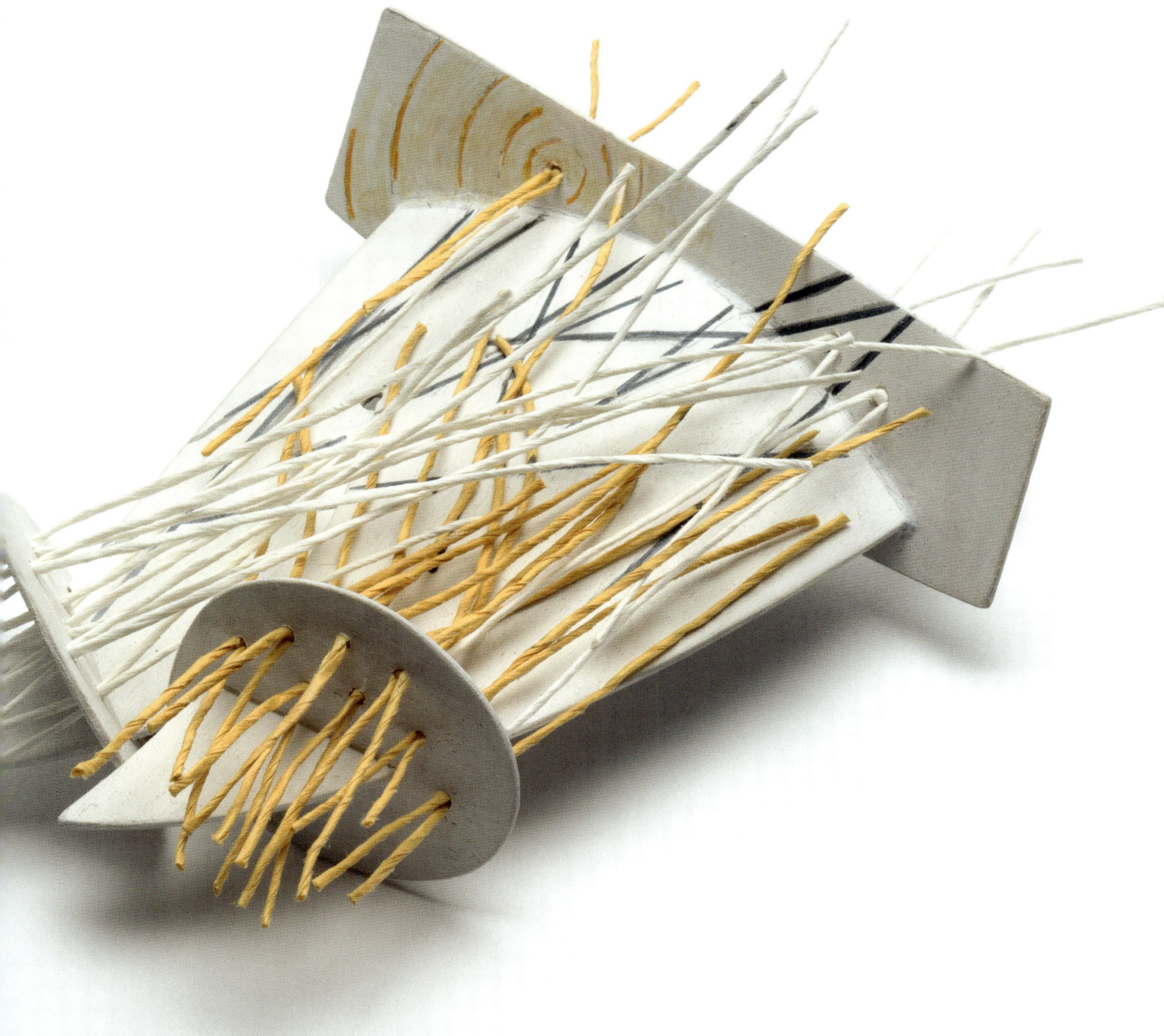

自由擷取線繩為主題創作,以及從自身觀點出發,法蘭茲·貝特一開始的選擇,其實是素材上所可以表達的品質: 線繩在圖解圖形上如同有生命般的結構,以及它可以表達漂浮或草圖感的特質。以自由擺盪為例,線繩其實是空無一物的空間與物體表面的連結,這些表面可以是透明塑膠或是上色的瓷物件。貝特使用短的線繩,不規律排列如破繭而出;但卻又在上下端相互交錯連結,同時具有實質與表徵上的意義。這些所有的元件組合起來可以是透視線圖的構圖,或是胸針相鄰空間的試驗草圖,但它們更是賞心悅目富有詩意的物件,甚至可以幻想解讀成大件的裝置藝術。

In a free adaptation of the cord as a theme and from his own point of view, Franz Bette initially uses the material's expressive qualities, the lifelike structure of the cord through its graphic path and the possibility to express something floating or sketch-like. In long free swings the cord connects empty space with a surface, which may be transparent plastic or painted porcelain. He uses short pieces of cord like hatching, arranged like loose bundles of strokes. At the same time they interlock at one end, joining above and below not only in reality but symbolically as well. These components generate compositions which might be perspectival study drawings or spatial sketches examining the subject of the space around the brooches, but they also set fantastic objects before our eyes which might as well be studies for large-scale installations.

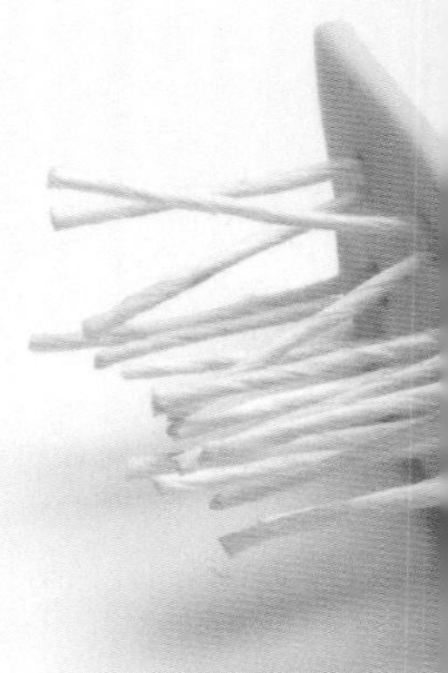

In einer freien Adaption des Themas Schnur nutzt Franz Bette zunächst den Ausdruck des Materials, die lebendige Struktur der Schnur und die Möglichkeit des zeichnerischen Verlaufs, um etwas Schwebendes, Skizzenhaftes zum Ausdruck zu bringen. Wie eine Linie verbindet die Schnur in langgezogenen, freien Schwüngen Leerräume mit Flächen, die aus transparentem Kunststoff oder bemaltem Porzellan sein können. Kurze Schnurabschnitte verwendet er wie Schraffuren, wie lose zu parallelen Strichbündeln geordnet. Gleichzeitig verschränken sie sich an einem Ende und verbinden nicht nur real, sondern auch sinnbildlich ein Oben und Unten. Diese Komponenten bilden Kompositionen aus, die perspektivisch Entwurfszeichnungen oder räumliche Skizzen sein können, die den Raum um das Thema Ansteckschmuck untersuchen, uns aber auch phantastische Körper vor Augen setzen, die Studien für großformatige Installationen sein könnten.

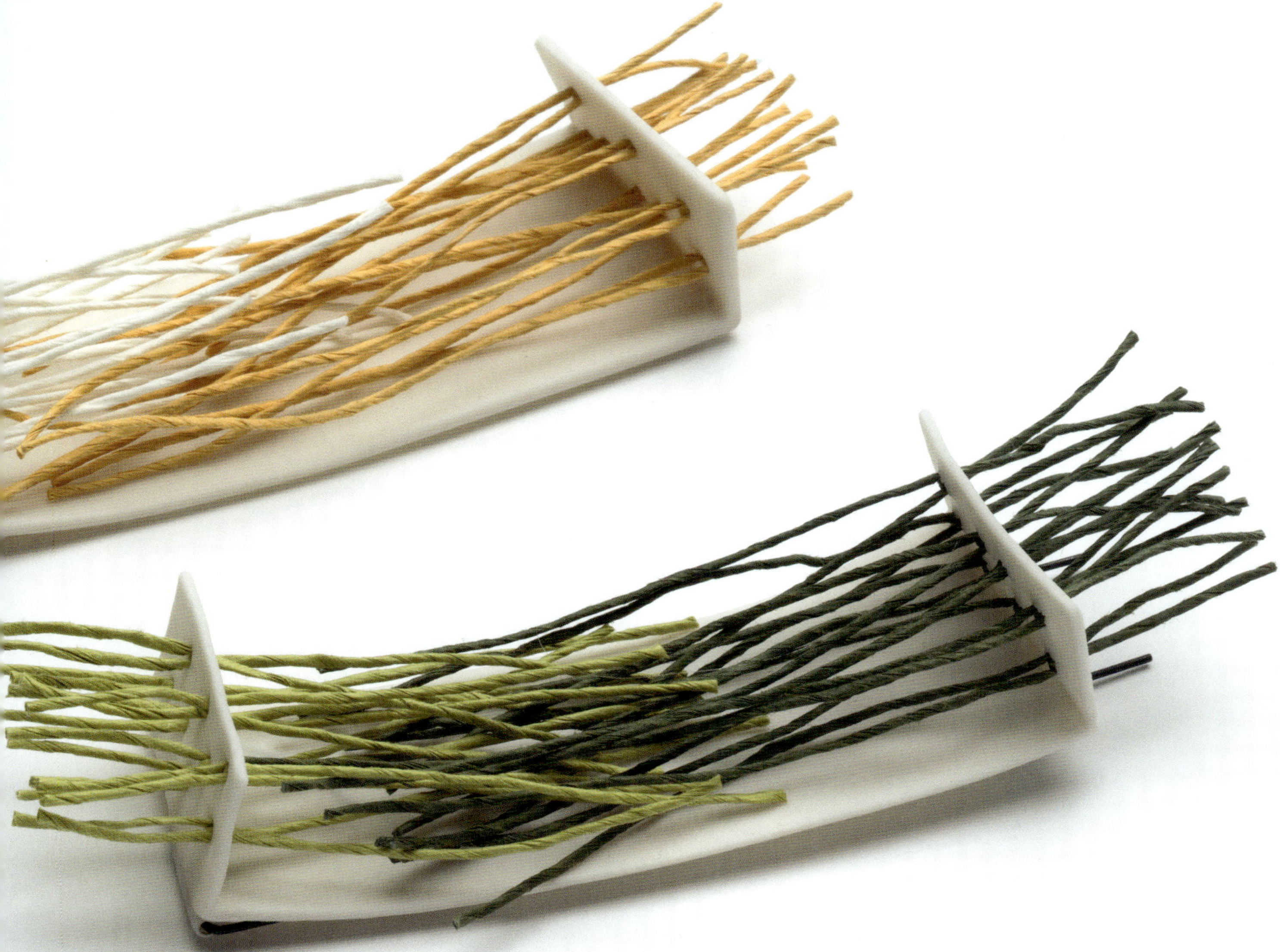

別針兩只，瓷，紙繩
2 Pins, porcelain, paper cord
2 Nadeln, Porzellan, Papierschnur
2018, 11 x 3 x 2 cm

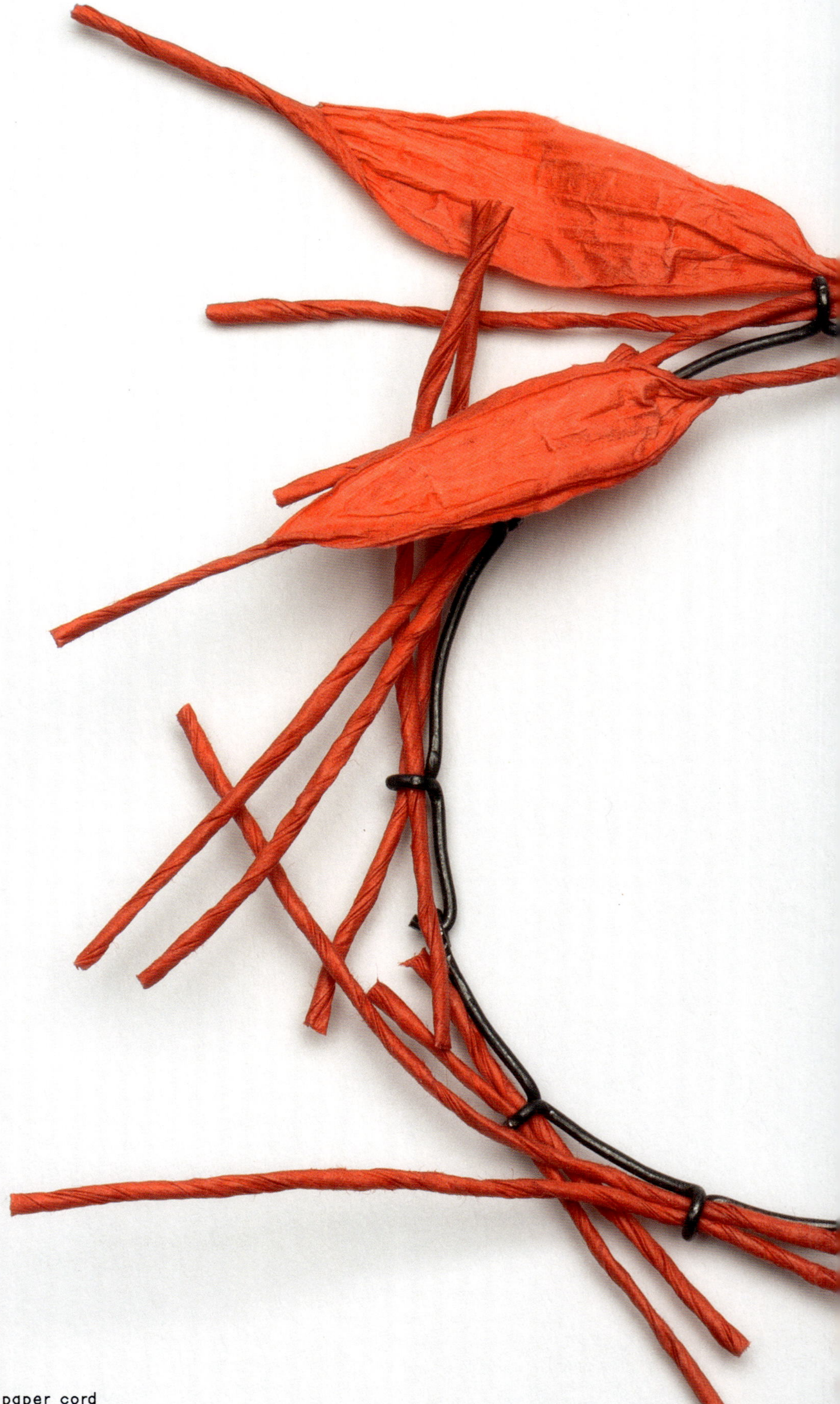

40

胸針, 低碳鋼絲, 紙繩
Brooch, mild steel wire, paper cord
Brosche, Eisendraht, Papierschnur
2018, 7 x 7 x 1 cm

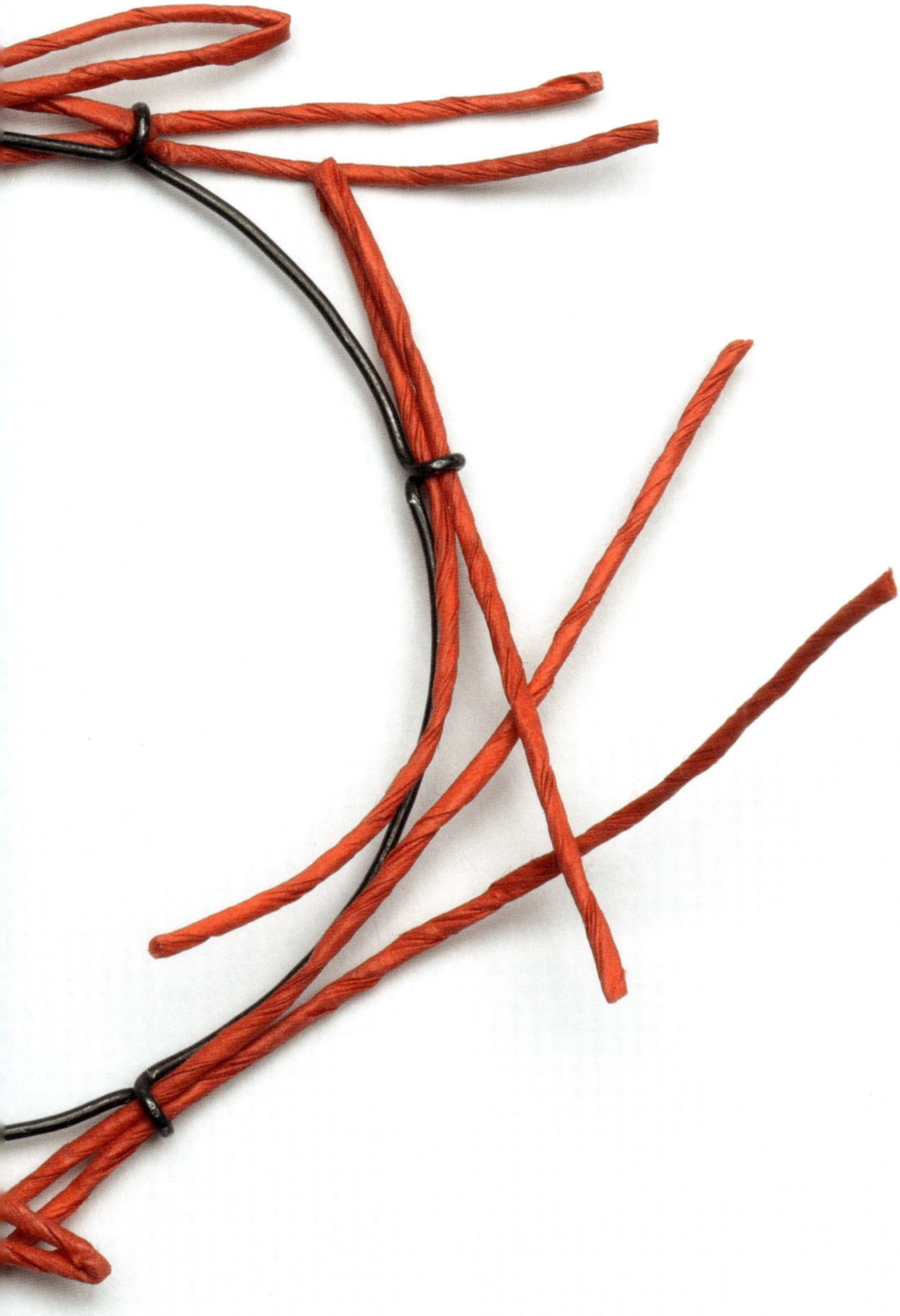

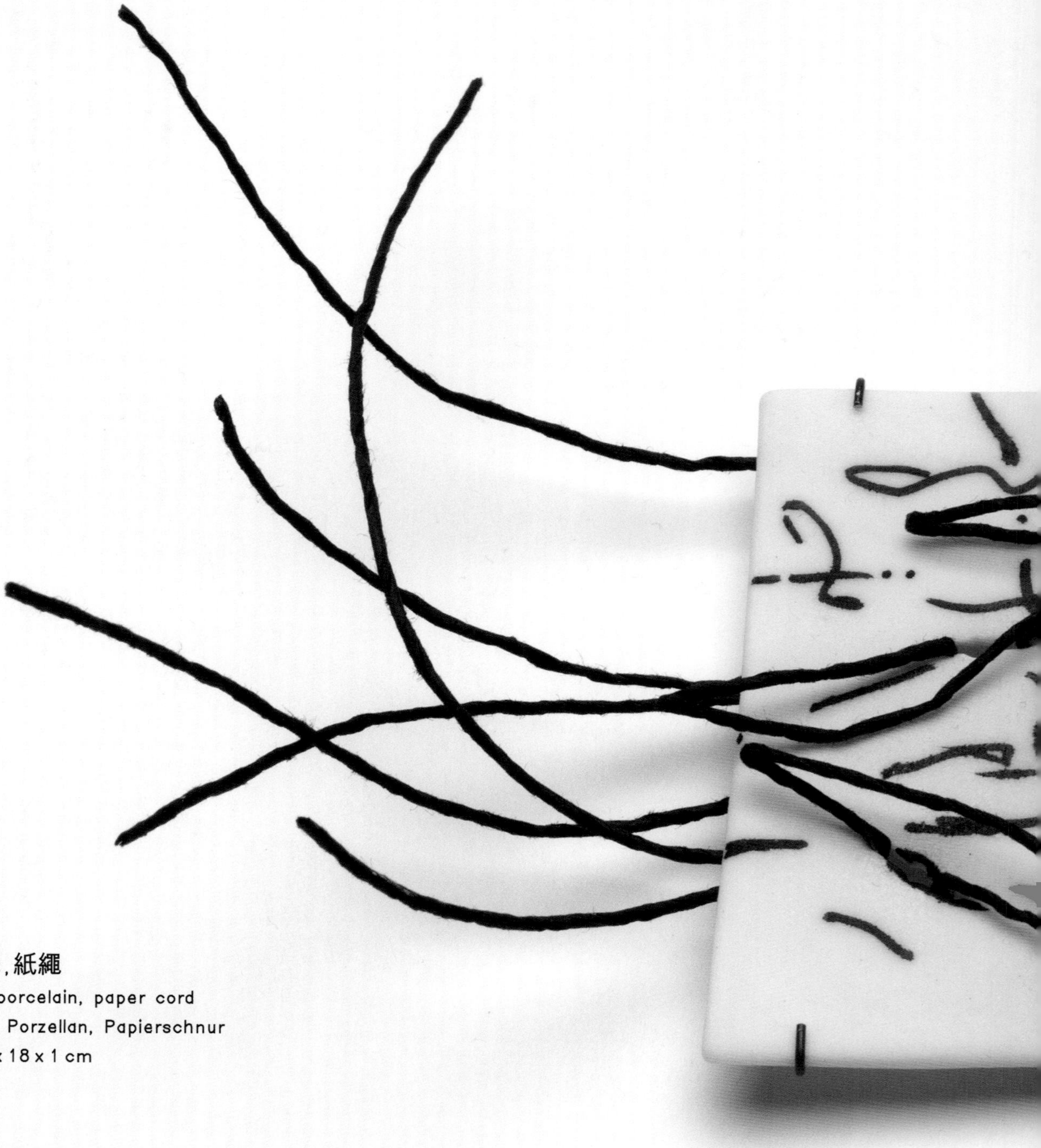

42

胸針,瓷,紙繩
Brooch, porcelain, paper cord
Brosche, Porzellan, Papierschnur
2018, 8 x 18 x 1 cm

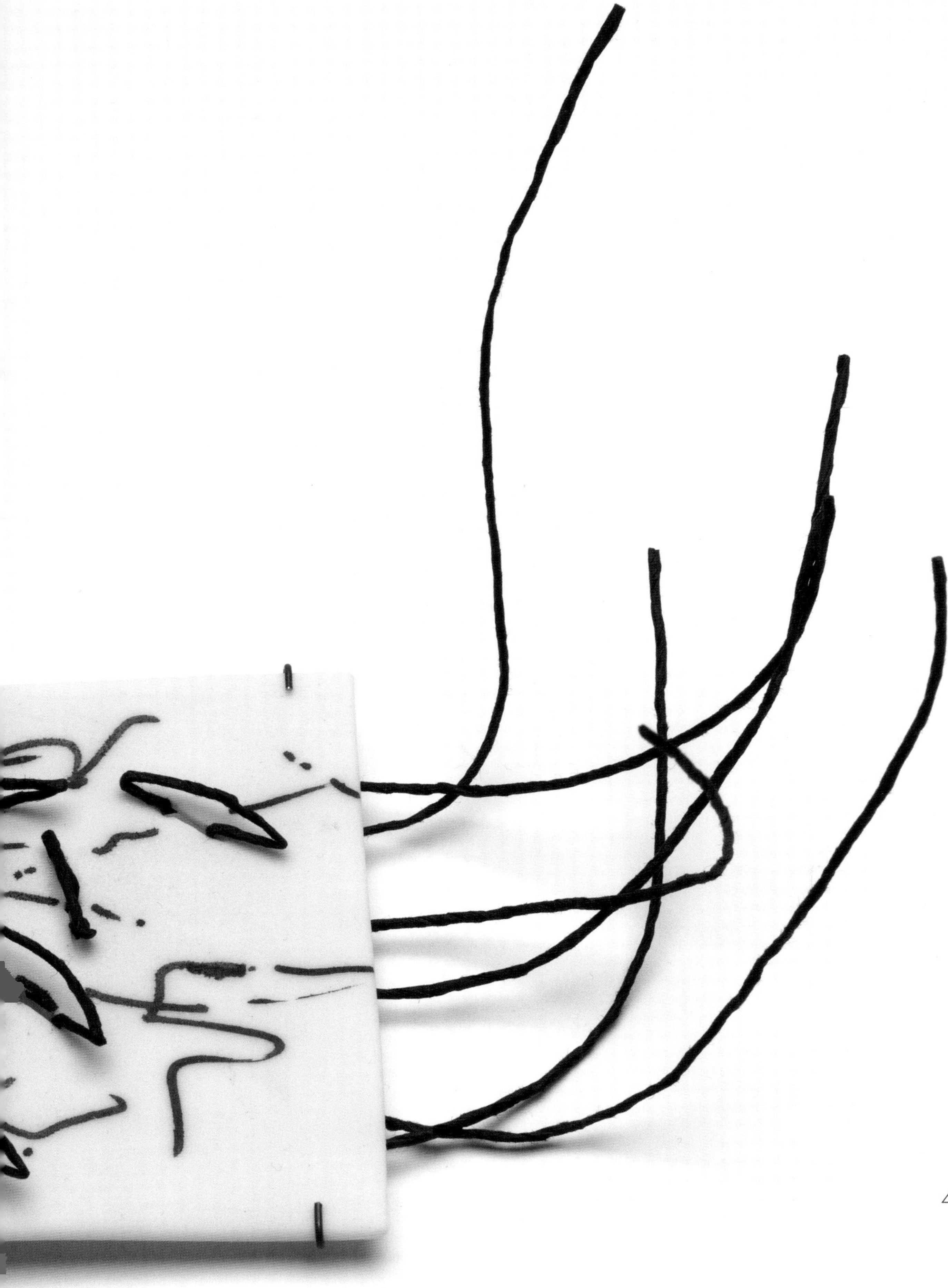

44

物件，亞麻布，環氧樹脂，木，石膏
Object, linen, epoxy, wood, plaster
Objekt, Leinen, Epoxidharz, Holz, Gips
2016, 18 x 10 x 5 cm

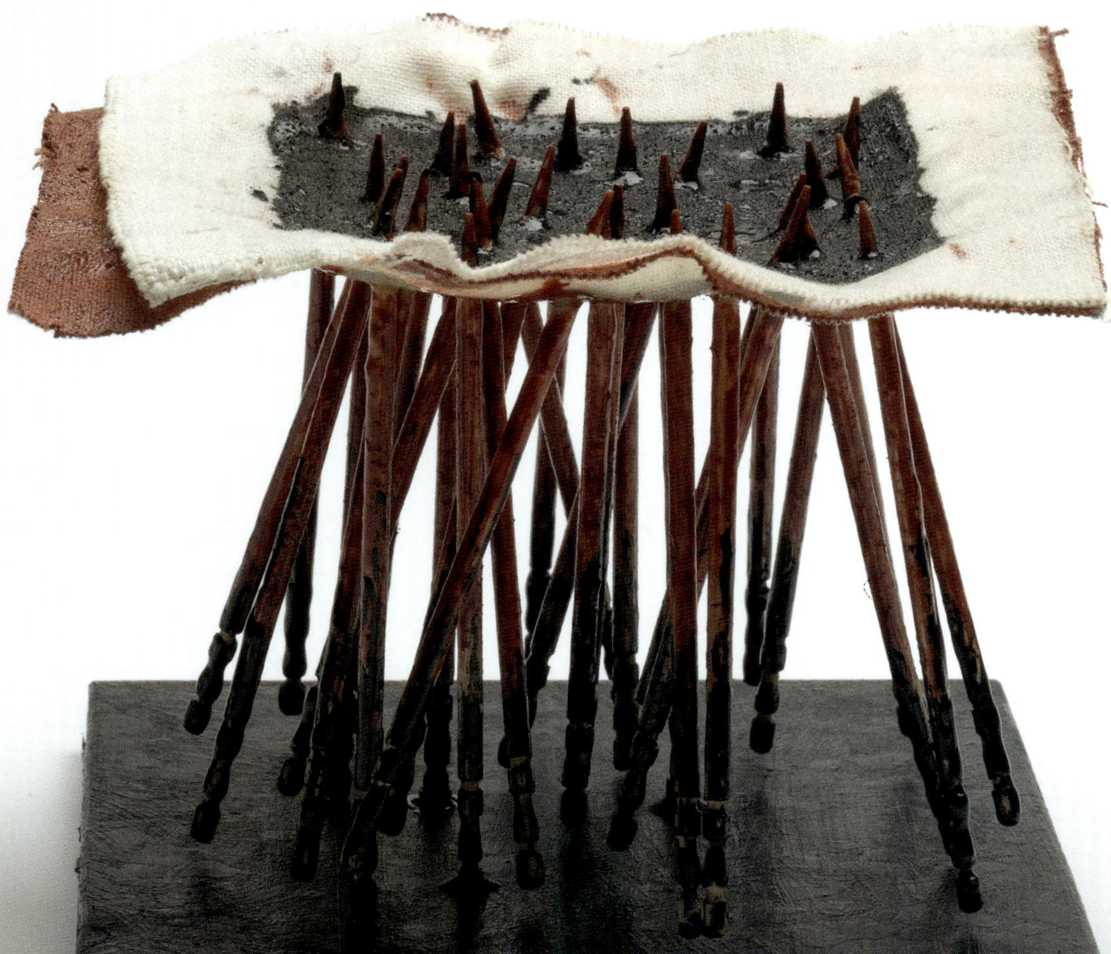

46

物件，低碳鋼絲，線繩，羊皮紙
Object, mild steel wire, cord, parchment
Objekt, Eisendraht, Schnur, Pergament
2012, 23 x 6 x 6 cm

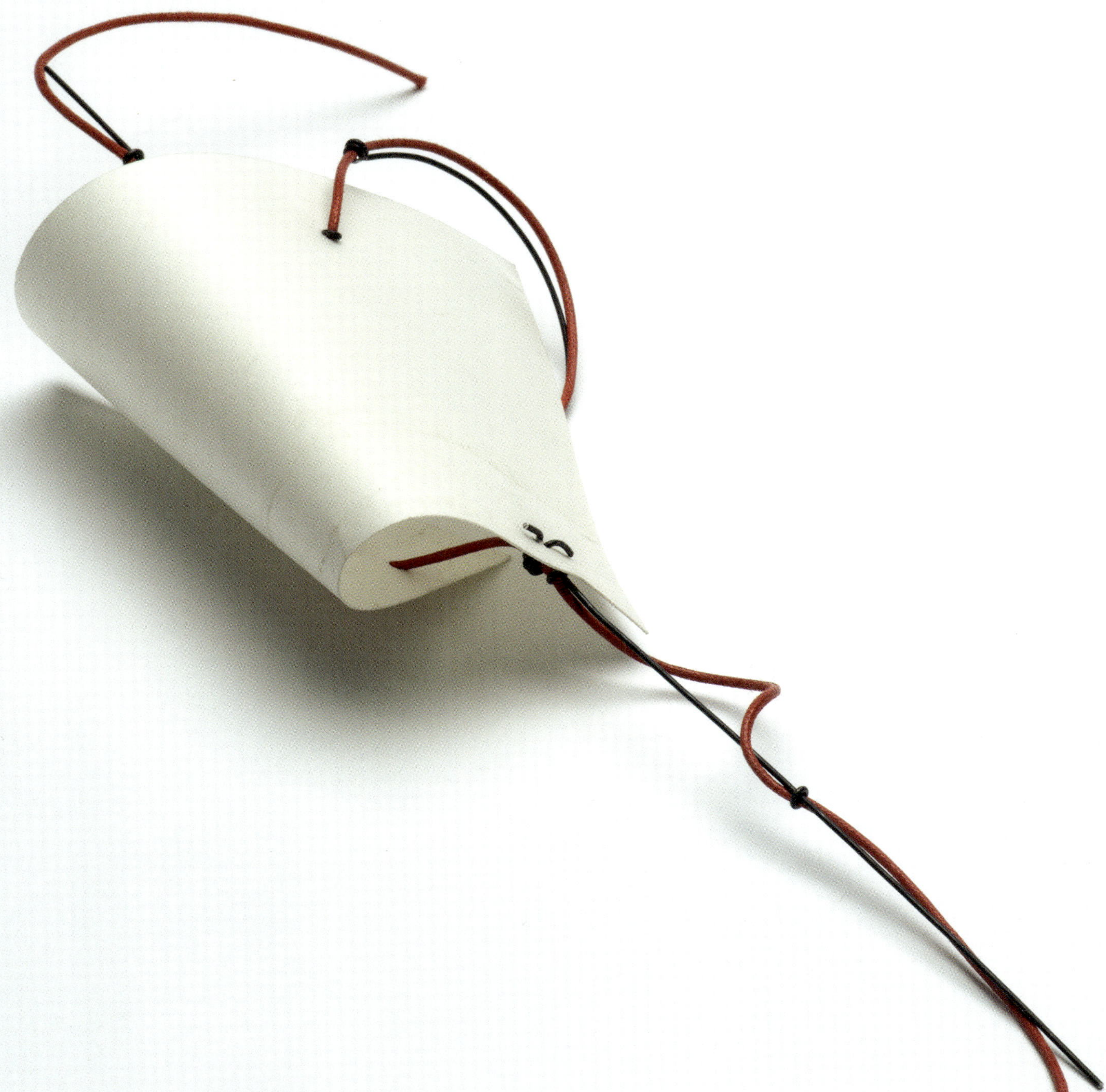

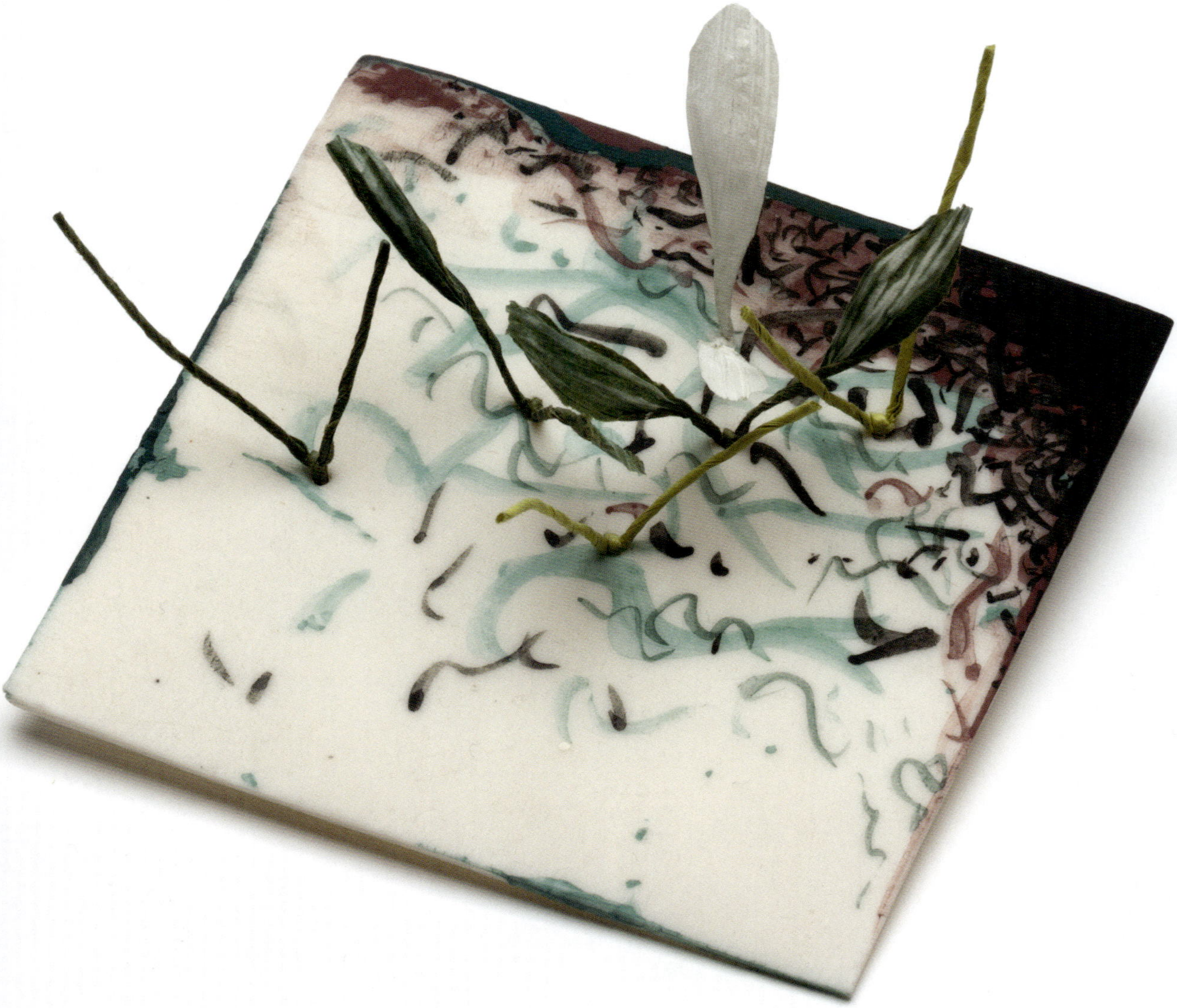

48

胸針,瓷,紙繩
Brooch, porcelain, paper cord
Brosche, Porzellan, Papierschnur
2018, 8 x 8 x 2 cm

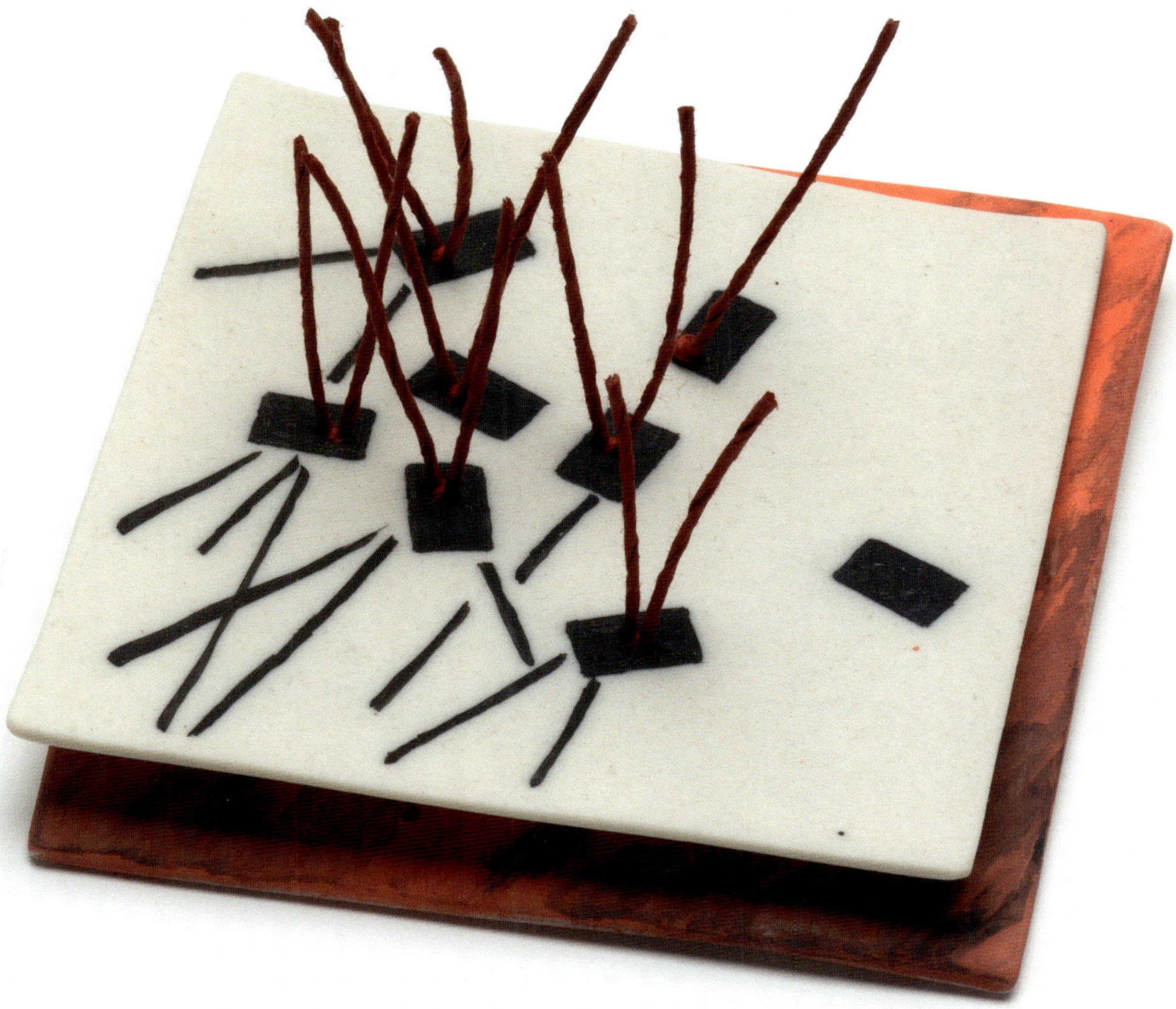

胸針，瓷，紙繩
Brooch, porcelain, paper cord
Brosche, Porzellan, Papierschnur
2018, 8 x 8 x 4 cm

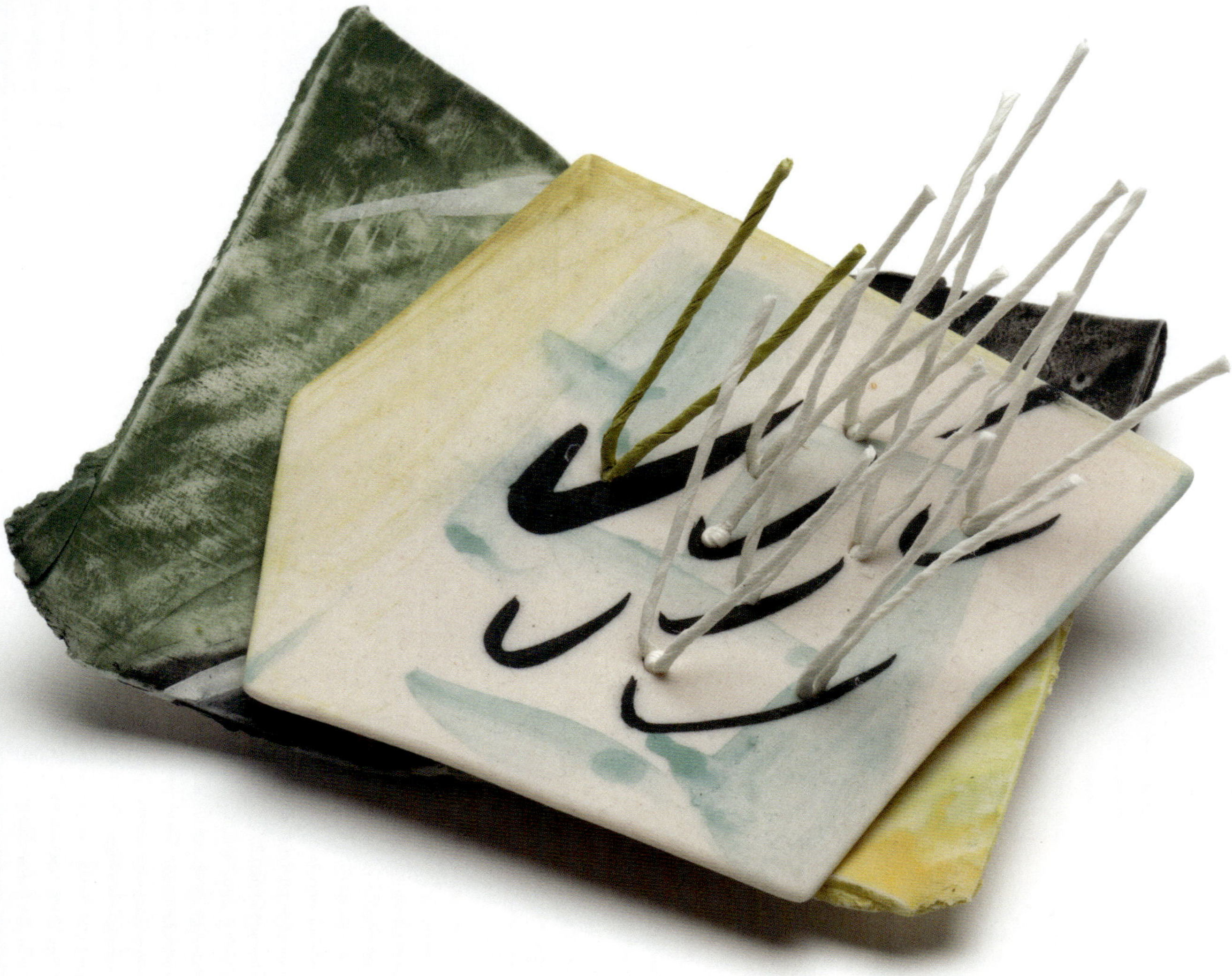

50 胸針,瓷,紙繩
Brooch, porcelain, paper cord
Brosche, Porzellan, Papierschnur
2018, 9 x 9 x 3.5 cm

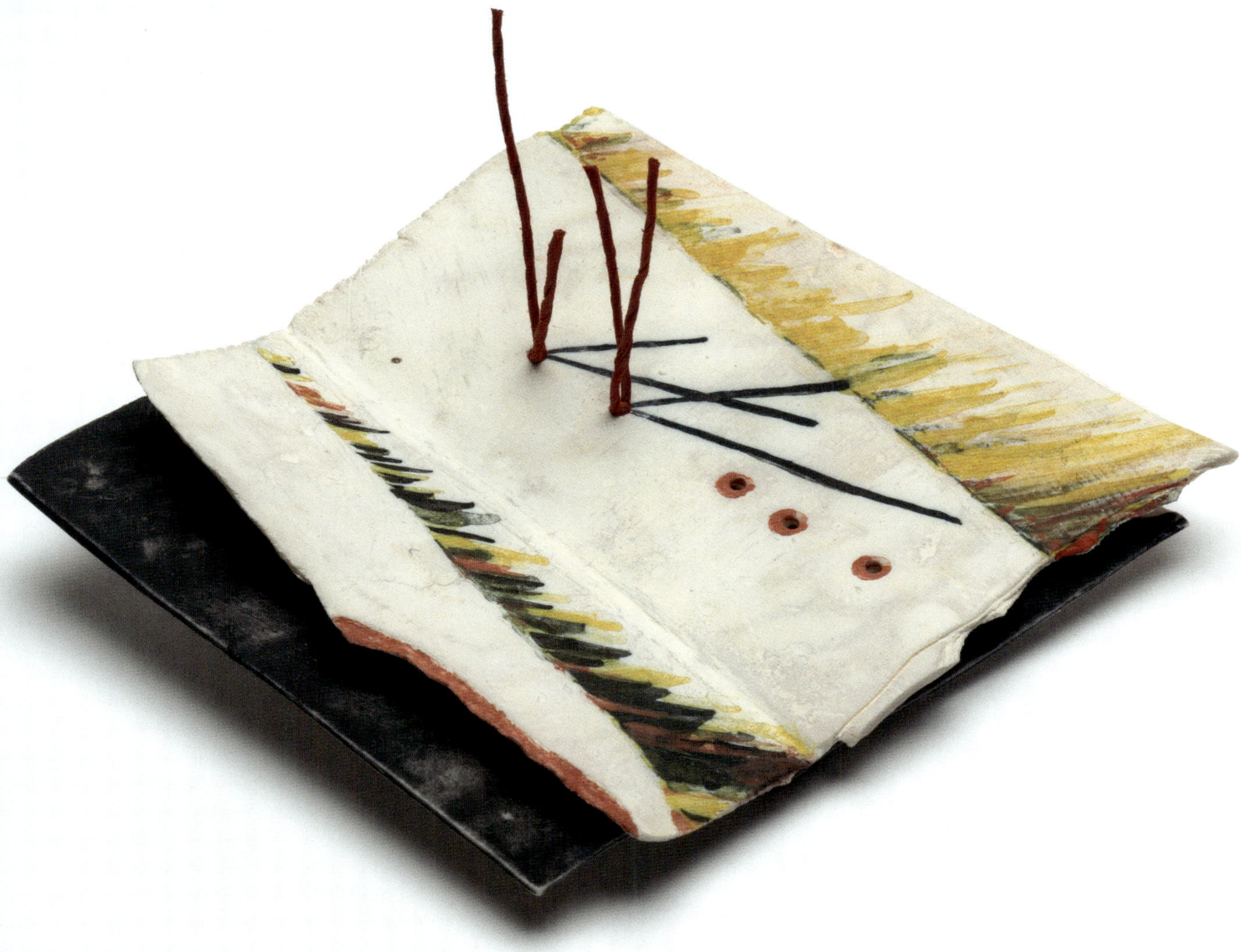

胸針,瓷,紙繩
Brooch, porcelain, paper cord
Brosche, Porzellan, Papierschnur
2018, 11 x 11 x 3.5 cm

形狀 – 顏色 – 符號

法蘭茲·貝特偏好可以在結構工序上以及在空間上,可以表達藝術性意圖的簡單形狀。莫比烏斯環、十字架、正圓形或是螺旋狀等具有高度符號意義的形體,都是他作品裡的規章教條。直到目前為止,色彩之於他在表達的選項裡多屬於抽象境界,如金屬、塑膠與貴重寶石的色譜範圍。這次他重新組織構圖,在瓷或竹的表面上如畫家般玩色。現在他的色彩從單色調的軸線發展延伸,顏色的轉換自然而然成為主角。自然色伴著純白的骨架結構,而一束束藍或綠、白或黃的短線圈,在空間裡附生鑲嵌。主角自然是紅線繩,移動自如開啟延續,或類似一具擁有著透明骨架的脊髓。

Form – Colour – Symbol

Franz Bette likes to work with forms whose simplicity assists his constructive working method and provides space to carry out his artistic intentions. The Möbius band, the cross, the circle or the spiral – forms with high symbolic value, belong to the formal canon of his work.[3] Until now colour appears in his expressive repertoire primarily in an abstract sense, in the colour spectrum of metals, plastic, and of precious stones. In his new compositions he tests colour playfully as a painter on porcelain or bamboo surfaces. Basically, however, his colour play is an expansion around the monochrome cord, which quite naturally takes over the role of colour transporter. Natural colours accompany white, skeletal forms. Bundles of cord segments in blue and green, or white and yellow embody spatial hatching. The main role, however, is played by the red cord, freely sweeping and an open continuation, or like a visible spinal cord within a transparent backbone.

[3] See S. Runde, Ornament without Ornament, Franz Bette Jeweller, Frankfurt am Main 2007.

52

物件,木,顏料,低碳鋼絲
Object, wood, paint, mild steel wire
Objekt, Holz, Farbe, Eisendraht
2017, 10 x 8 x 2 cm

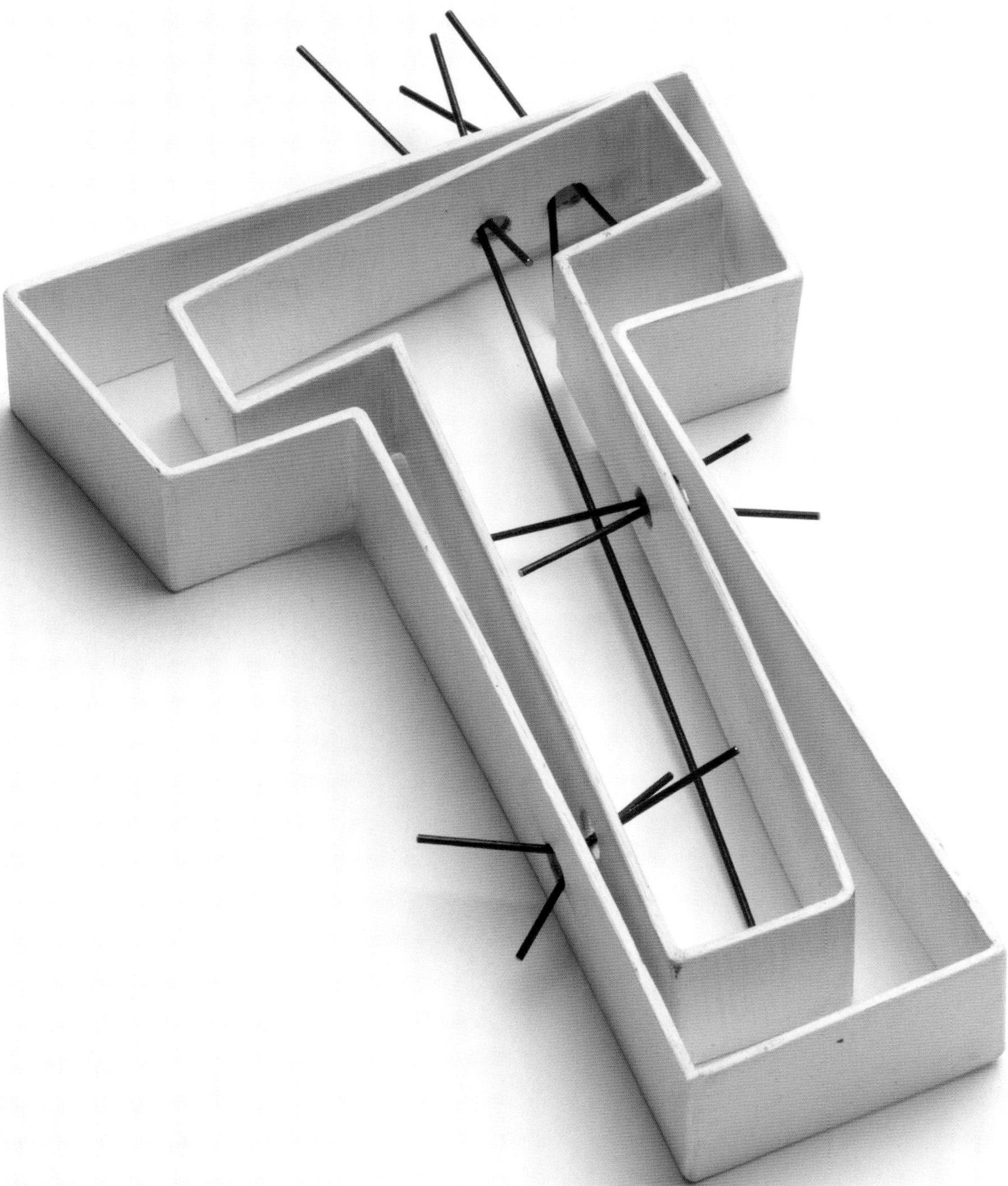

Form – Farbe – Symbol

Franz Bette operiert gern mit Formen, die in ihrer Einfachheit seine konstruktive Vorgehensweise unterstützen und außerdem Raum und Flächen bieten, seine gestalterischen Intentionen zu verwirklichen. Die Lemniskate, das Kreuz, der Kreis oder die Spirale, Formen mit hohem Symbolcharakter, gehören in den Formenkanon seines Werks.[3] Farbe tritt im Ausdrucksrepertoire von Franz Bette bisher schwerpunktmäßig abstrakt im Farbspektrum der Metalle, Kunststoffe und der edlen Steine auf. In seinen neuen Kompositionen erprobt er Farbe malerisch, spielerisch auf Porzellan- oder Bambusflächen. Wesentlich erweitert sich dieses Farbspiel aber um die einfarbige Schnur, die ganz ungezwungen und selbstverständlich die Rolle eines Farbträgers übernimmt. Naturfarben begleitet sie weiße, skelettartige Formen. Bündel aus blauen und grünen oder weißen und gelben Schnurabschnitten verkörpern räumliche Schraffuren. Die Hauptrolle spielt jedoch die rote Schnur, als freier Schwung weich und offen auslaufend oder wie ein Spinalkanal im inneren der Wirbelsäule.

[3] Siehe dazu S. Runde, Franz Bette, Schmuck – Ornament ohne Ornament, Frankfurt am Main 2007

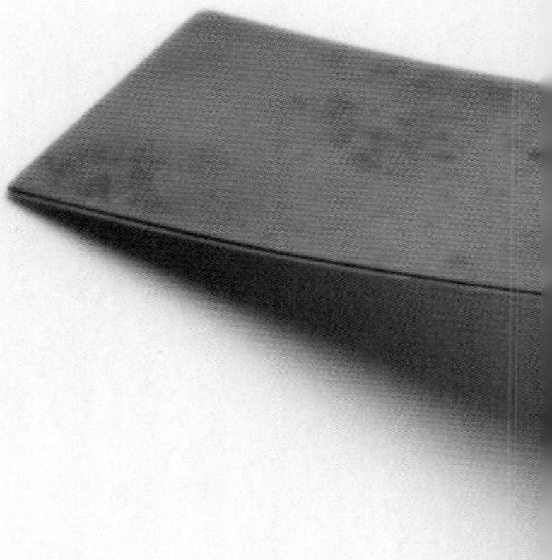

戒指,不鏽鋼,純金,鈀金
Ring, stainless steel, fine gold, palladium
Ring, Edelstahl, Feingold, Palladium
1988, 3 x 10 cm
Schmuckmuseum Pforzheim, Germany

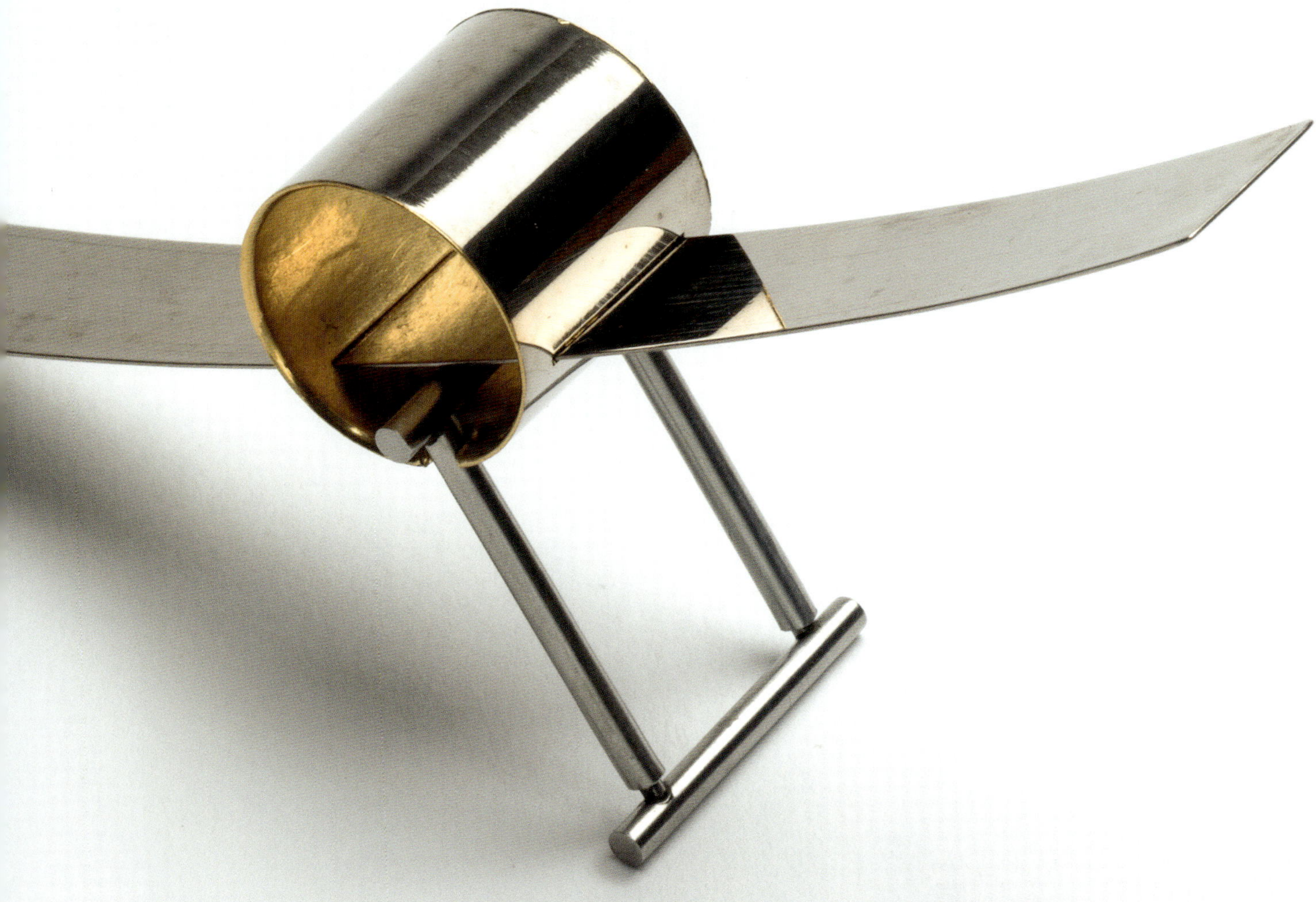

棉布,針,線
Cotton fabric, needle, thread
Baumwollgewebe, Nähnadel, Faden

56

物件,厚描圖紙,紙繩
Object, transparent paper, paper cord
Objekt, Transparentpapier, Papierschnur
2018, 10 x 8 x 8 cm

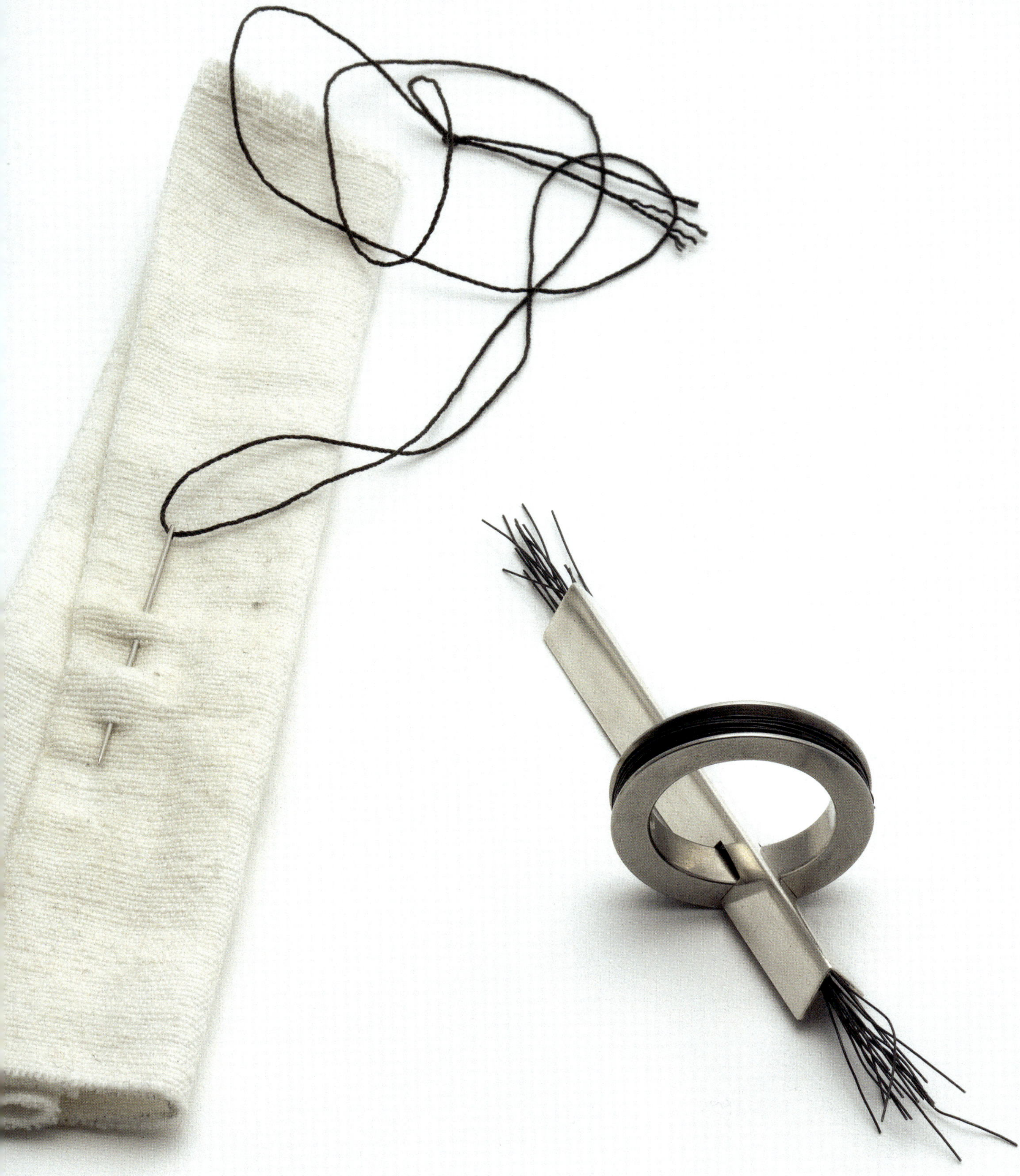

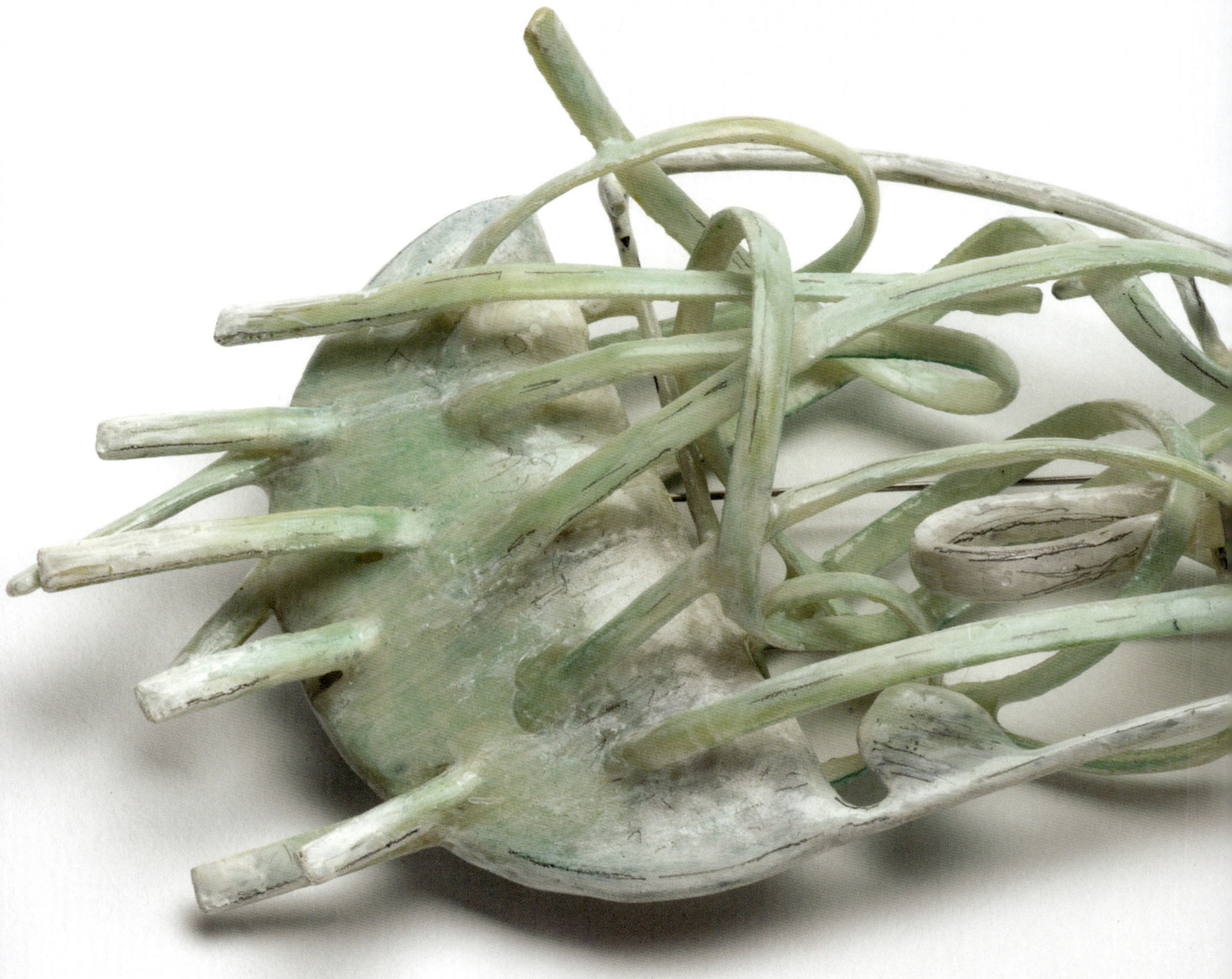

58 胸針，帆布，環氧樹脂，色粉，低碳鋼絲
Brooch, canvas, epoxy, pigment, mild steel wire
Brosche, Leinwand, Epoxidharz, Pigment, Eisendraht
2017, 14 x 8 x 2.5 cm

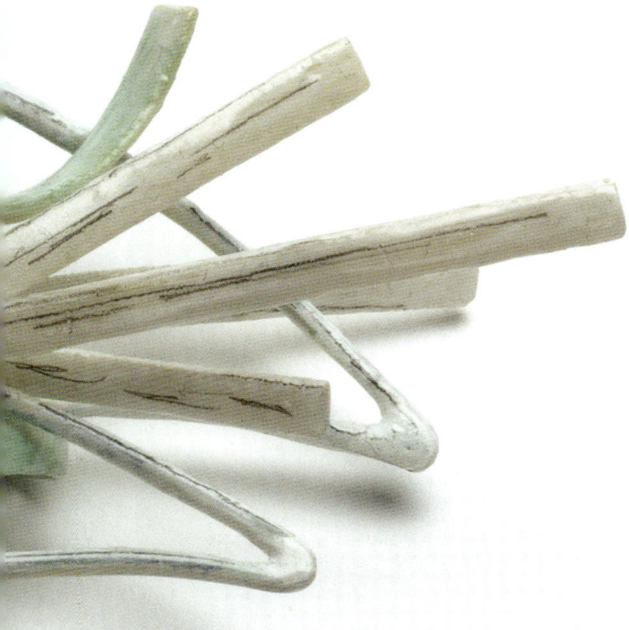

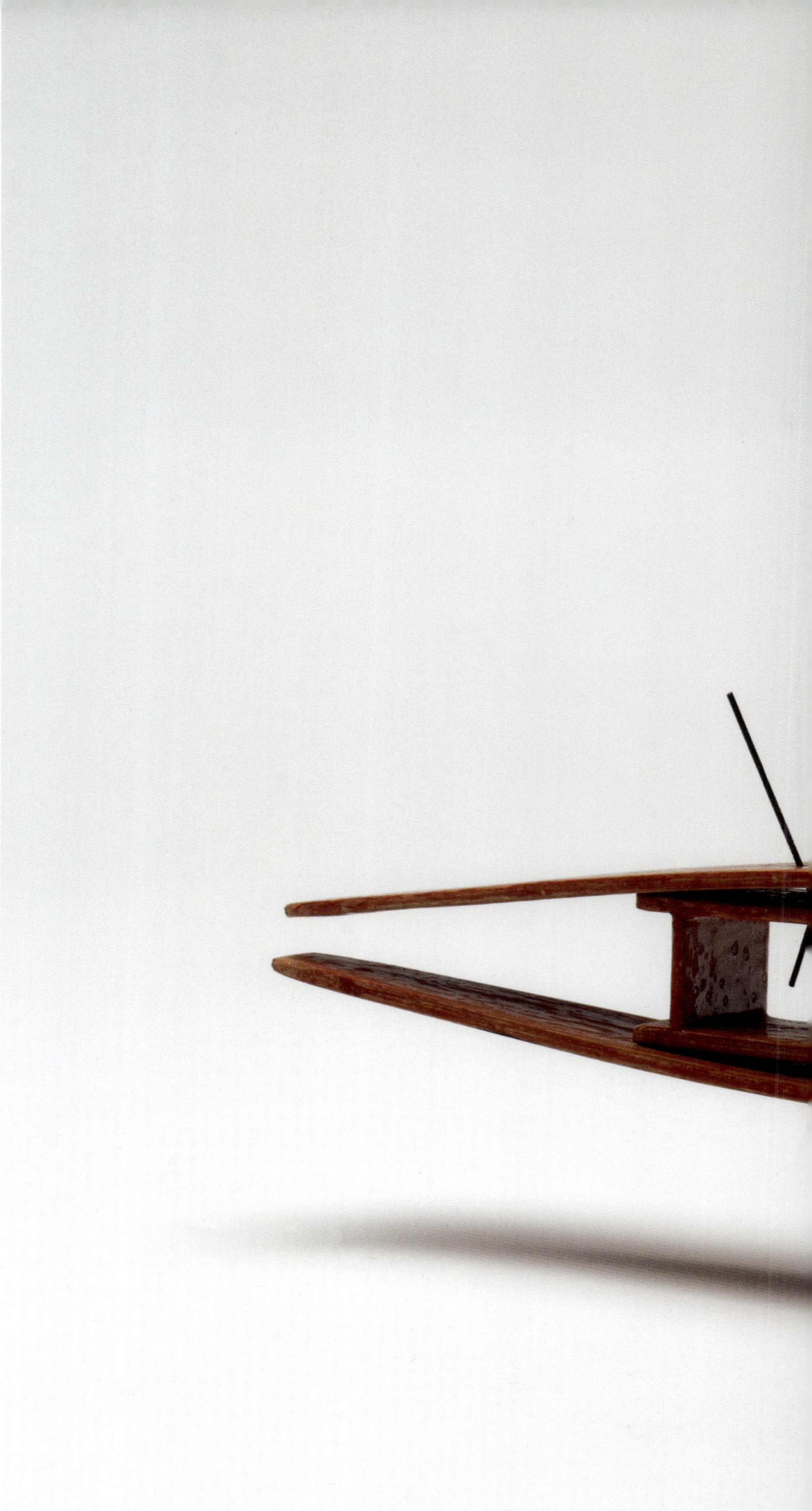

60 物件，竹，環氧樹脂，低碳鋼絲
Object, bamboo, epoxy, mild steel wire
Objekt, Bambus, Epoxidharz, Eisendraht
2018, 22 x 6 x 4 cm

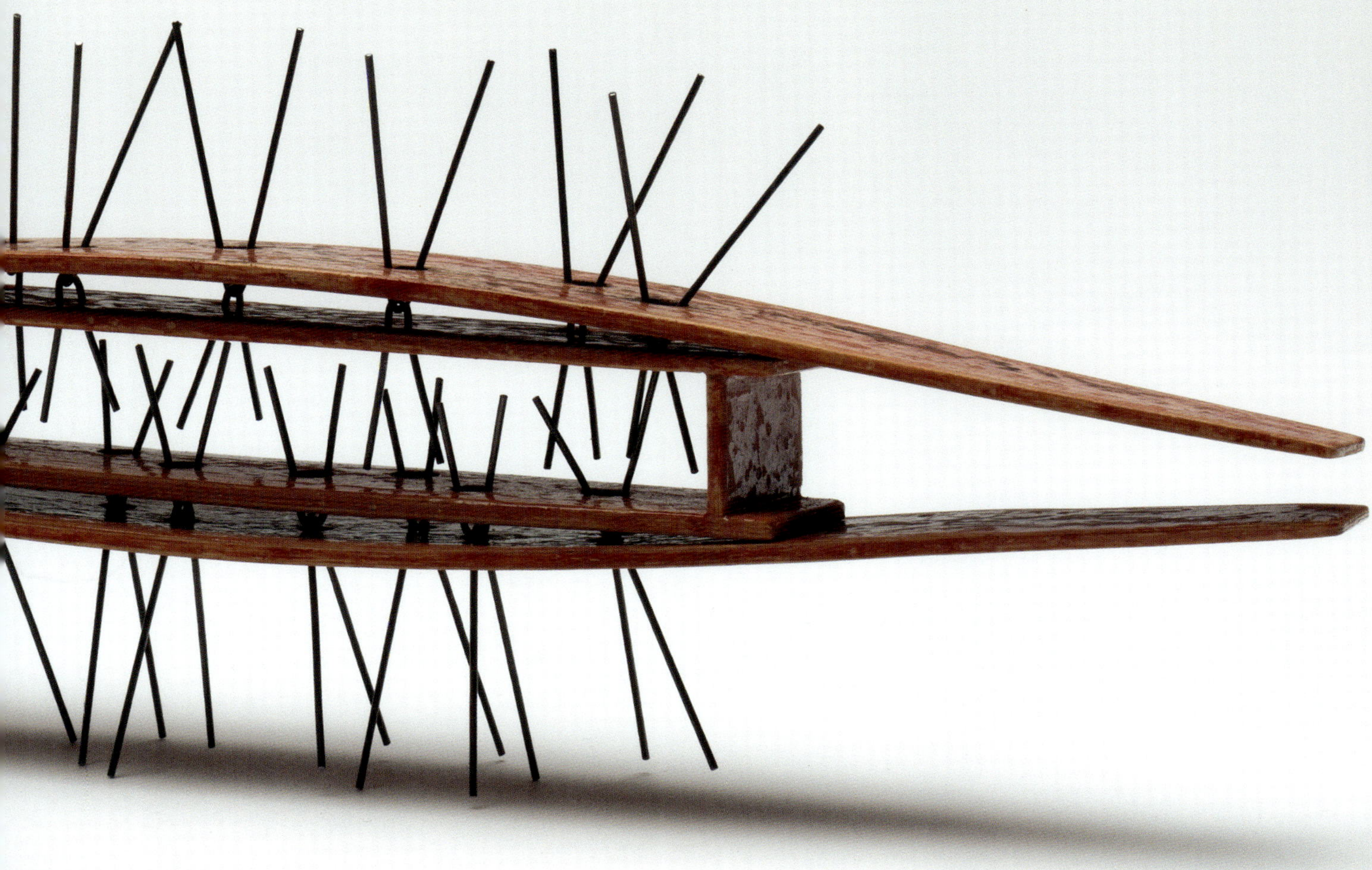

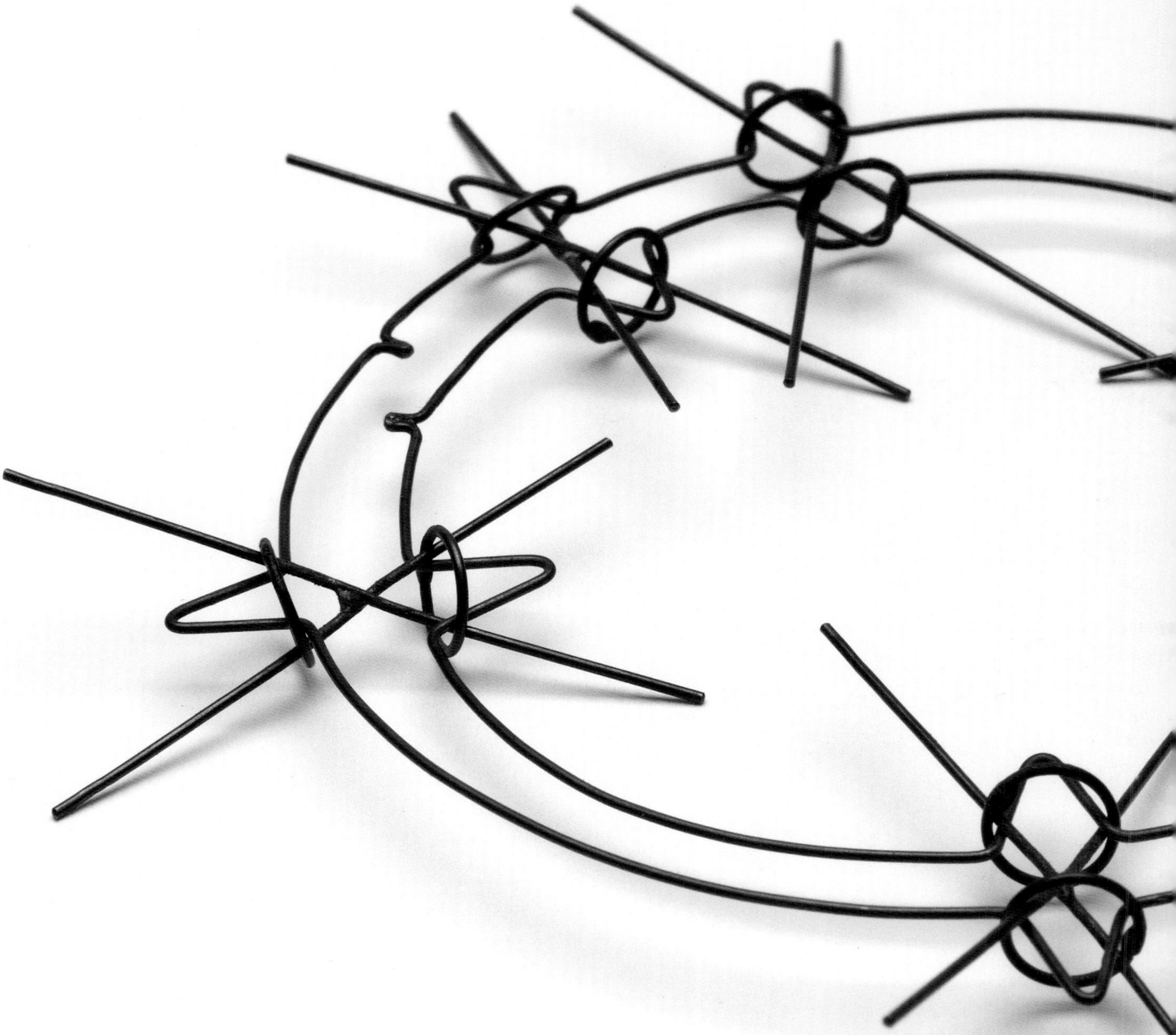

62
物件，低碳鋼絲
Object, mild steel wire
Objekt, Eisendraht
2007, 10 x 0.8 cm

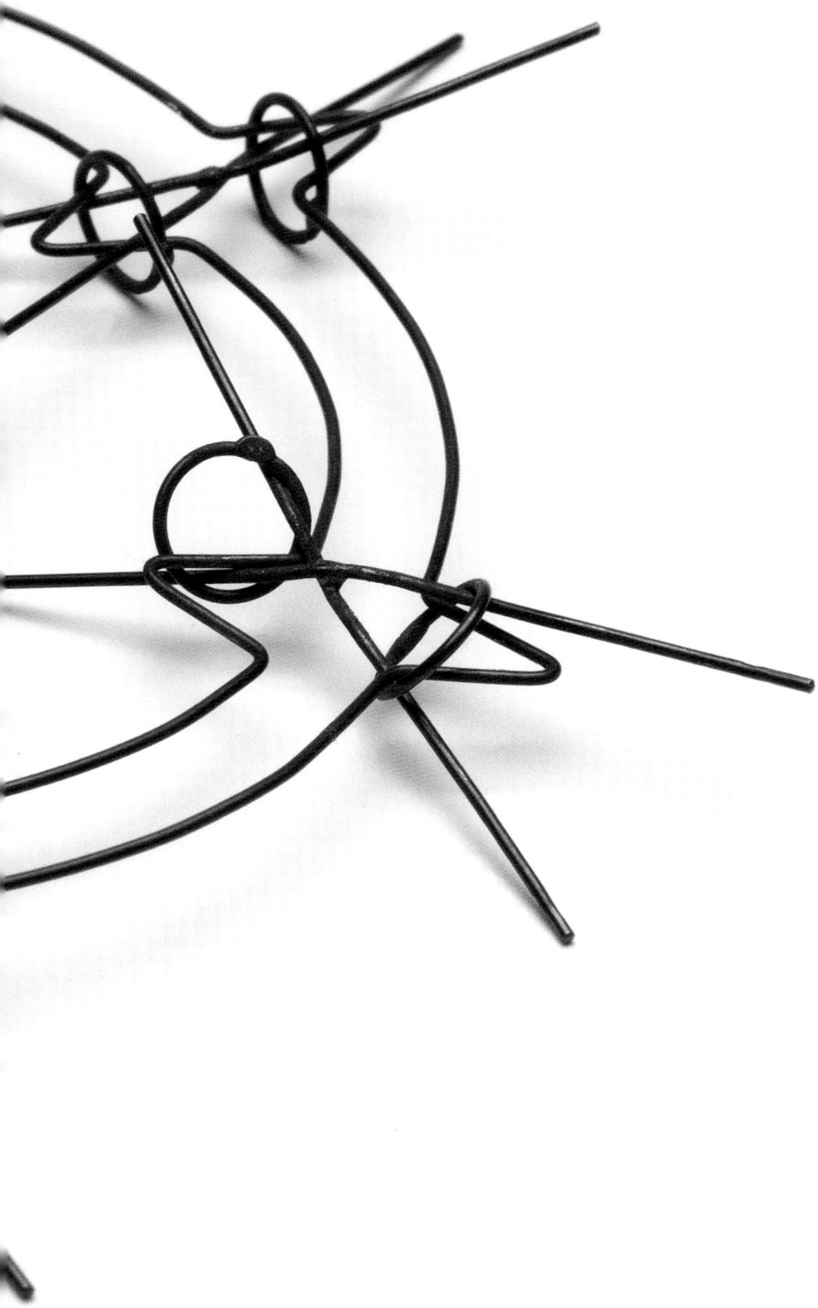

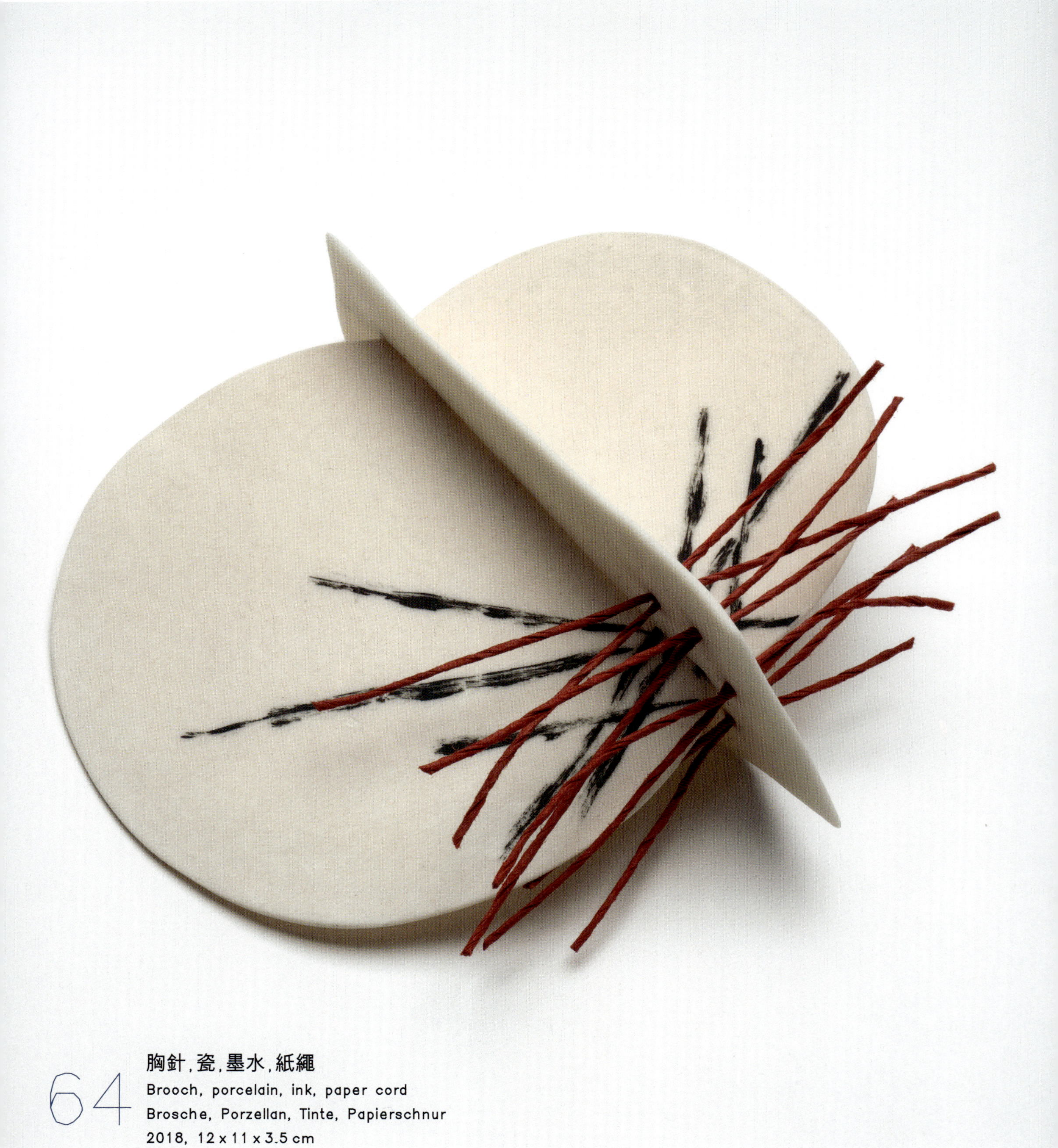

64

胸針,瓷,墨水,紙繩
Brooch, porcelain, ink, paper cord
Brosche, Porzellan, Tinte, Papierschnur
2018, 12 x 11 x 3.5 cm

顏色與形狀在所有文化裡都代表意義。它們的隱喻如同暗潮,如何解讀都與每位觀者獨有的角度相關。除了法蘭茲·貝特在先前的創作上所使用的符號形狀,及後來選擇使用的新元素與材質: 竹子、瓷跟線繩的觀點,對亞洲文化來說也非常吸引人。鋼絲與線繩彼此互動,打開了觀看的新方式, 也相互印證符號表徵程度的意義。色彩的角色變得新鮮少見。主角是紅色, 特別是以繩結模式, 強化了東西方的文化轉移。紅色這個幸運的使者在西方文化也同樣承載著意義:主要為統治者的顏色。紅色是皇室的屬色, 正因為是紅色顏料的稀少性與價值。對平民百姓來講, 色紅如血恐怕是最直接的聯想了。

Colour and form carry meanings in all cultures. Their respective metaphorical meaning is present as an undercurrent whose relevance depends on the particular perspective of the viewer. In addition to the previous symbolic forms in Franz Bette's work, it is appealing to discover these newly chosen elements and materials – bamboo, porcelain and the cord – with a view to Asian culture. They interact with each other and open the way for new perceptions as well as levels of symbolic meaning as exemplified by the steel wire and the cord. The role of colour also comes to be newly seen. The central role of the colour red, especially taken on by the cord, intensifies the cultural shift between East and West. Red, the bringer of luck, is also laden with meaning in Western culture, where it is primarily a dominator. Red is the colour of royalty, also because of the rarity and value of the pigment. Common to all people is the fundamental association with red as the colour of blood.

Form und Farbe sind in allen Kulturen Bedeutungsträger. Als Unterton schwingt der ihnen zugedachte metaphorische Sinn jeweils mit und ist für unterschiedliche Rezeptionsperspektiven von Relevanz. Es hat seinen Reiz, neben den bisherigen Symbolformen im Werk von Bette diese neuen, mit Blick auf die asiatische Kultur ausgewählten Materialien und Elemente wie Bambus, Porzellan und die Schnur zu entdecken. Sie interagieren und eröffnen neue Wahrnehmungen und auch symbolische Bedeutungsebenen. Am Beispiel von Stahldraht und der Schnur lässt sich dies exemplarisch nachvollziehen. Auch die Rolle der Farbe tritt neu in den Blick. Die zentrale Rolle der Farbe Rot, die insbesondere die Schnur übernimmt, verstärkt diesen *cultural shift* zwischen West und Ost. Das glücksbringende Rot ist auch in der westlichen Kultur mit symbolischer Bedeutung hinterlegt. Hier ist Rot vor allem eine Dominante, Rot ist eine königliche Farbe, und dies auch aufgrund der ursprünglichen Seltenheit und der damit verbundenen Kostbarkeit des Färbestoffs. Verbindend bleibt die elementare Bedeutung des Blutes.

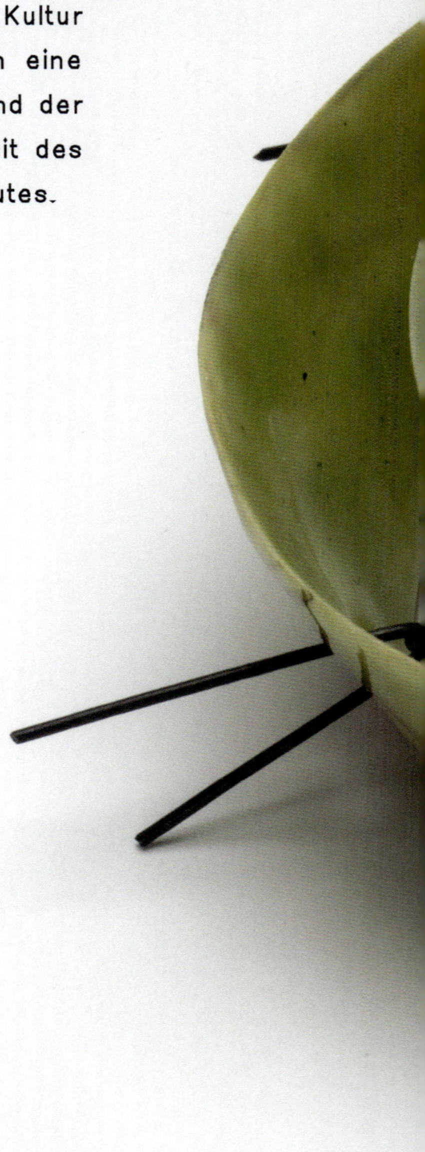

物件,厚描圖紙,環氧樹脂,顏料,低碳鋼絲
Object, transparent paper, epoxy, paint, mild steel wire
Objekt, Transparentpapier, Epoxidharz, Farbe, Eisendraht
2017, 9 x 8 x 2.5 cm

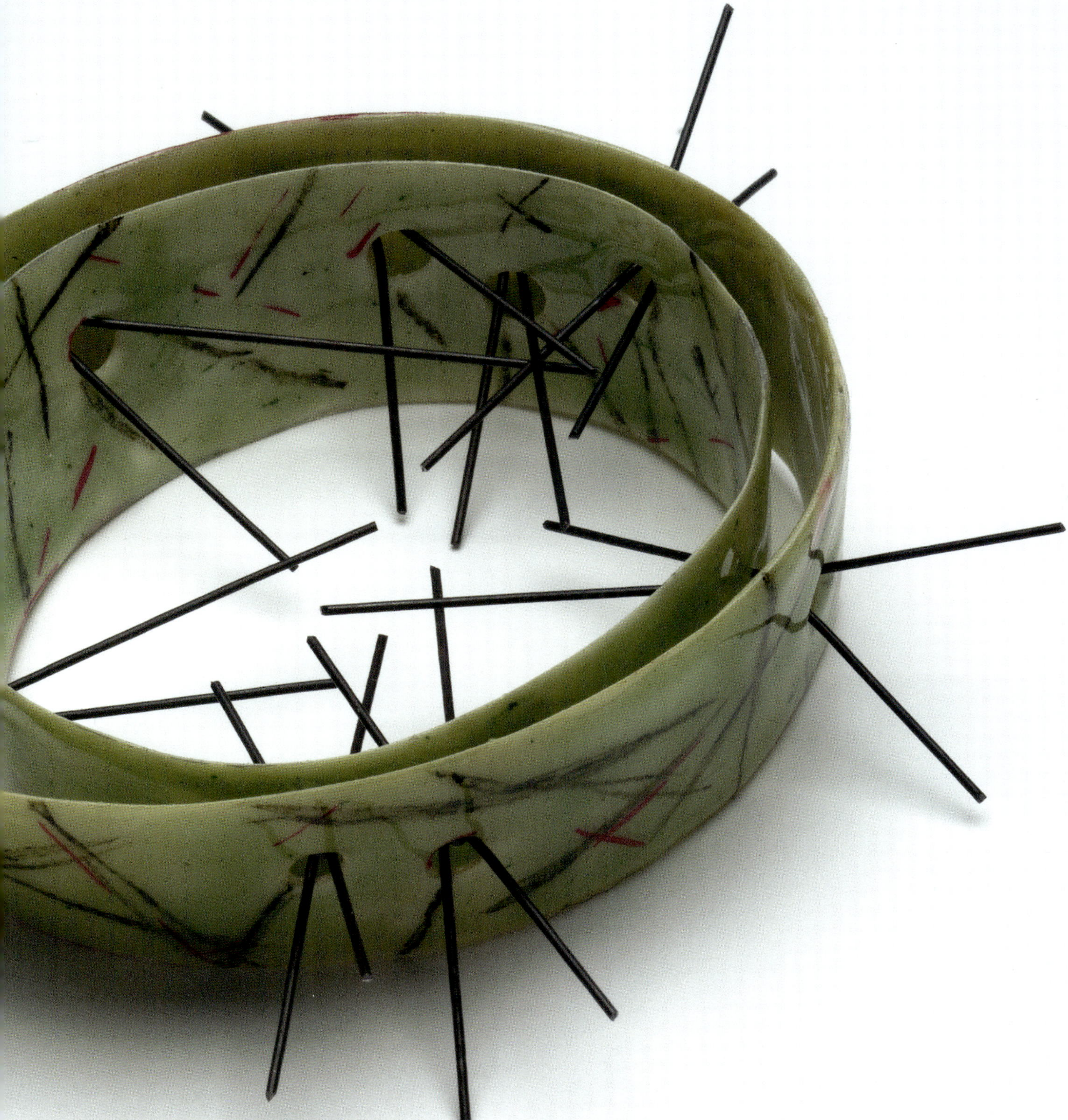

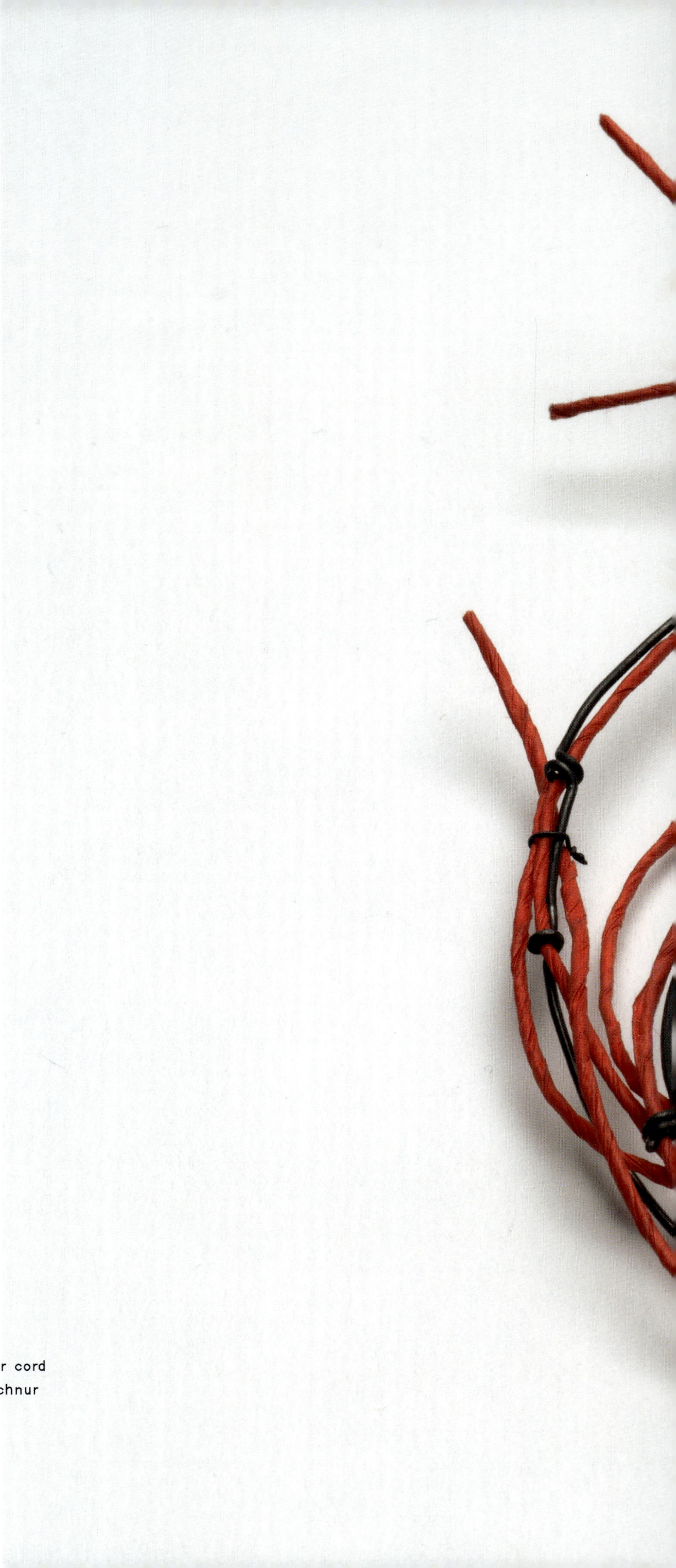

68 胸針，低碳鋼絲，紙繩
Brooch, mild steel wire, paper cord
Brosche, Eisendraht, Papierschnur
2018, 7 x 7 x 1 cm

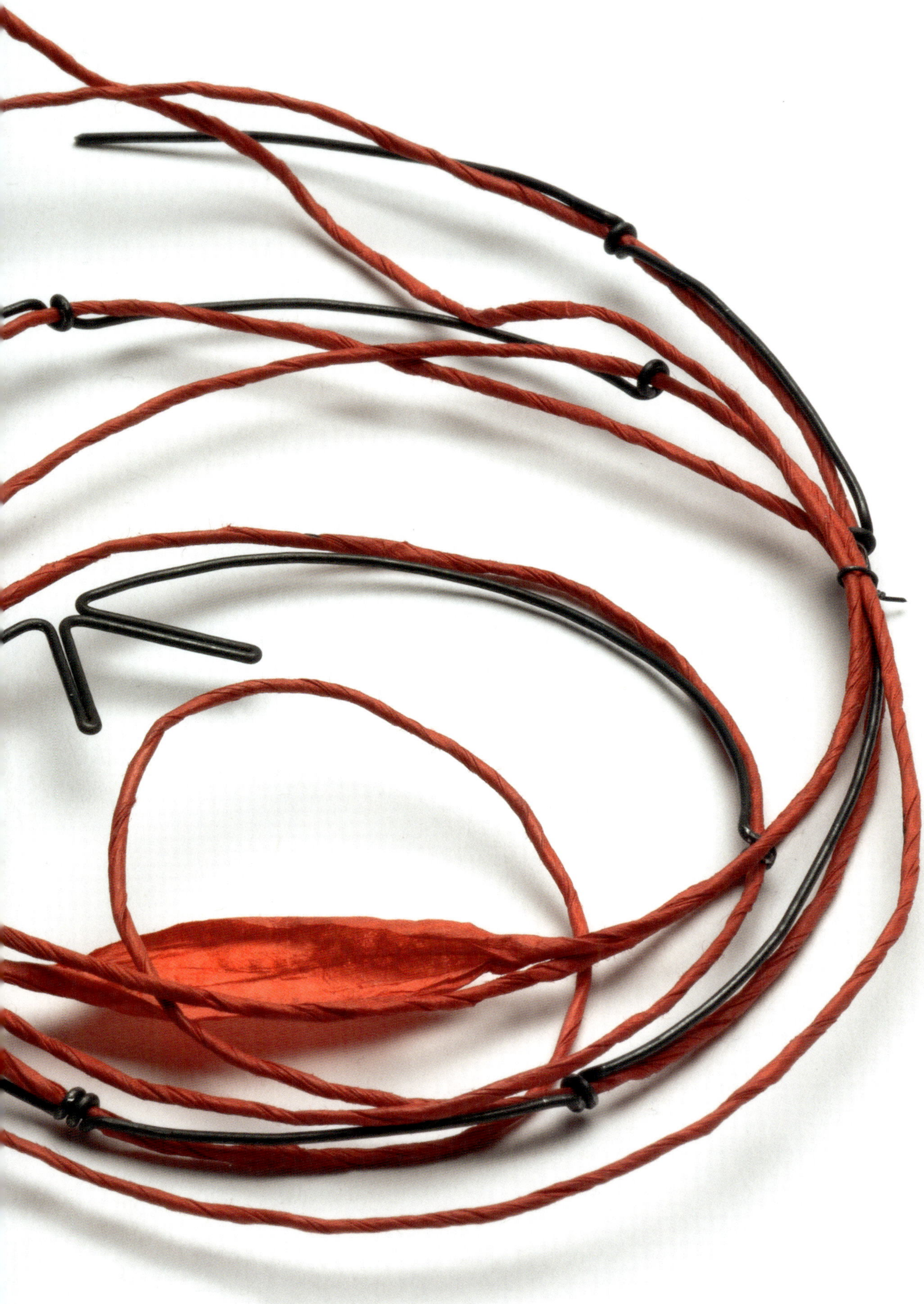

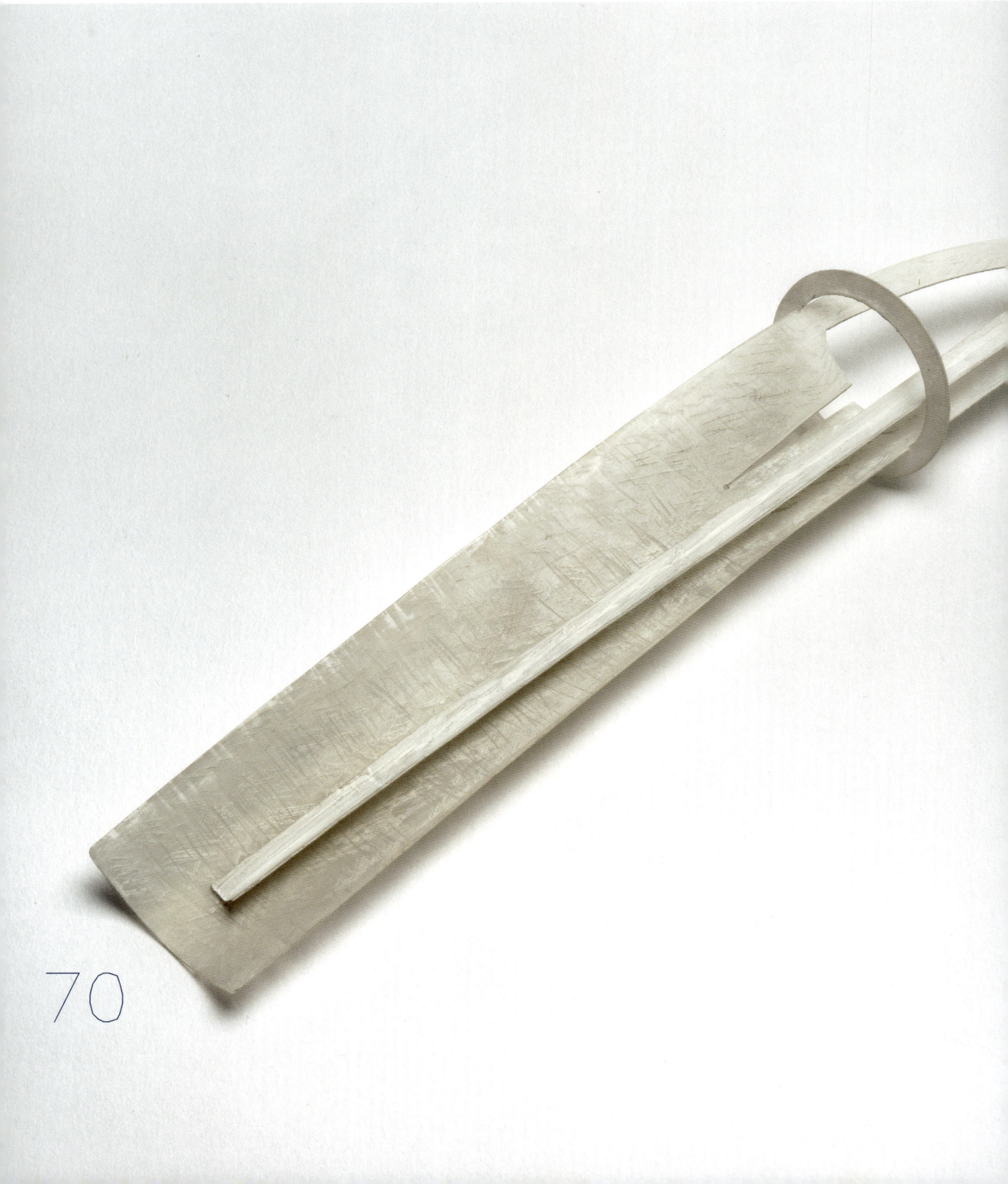

物件，塑膠，顏料
Object, plastic, paint
Objekt, Kunststoff, Farbe
2012, 15 x 5 x 3 cm

結語

法蘭茲·貝特將自己全神投入這系列的新創作,滿注著玩趣的熱情與新體驗的刺激,而他也開啟了一個新的、未完成的過程。創作初始他對於處理技術性高難度的金屬材質部分(特別是鋼),使之成為輕浮自在是無法克服的；後來經由靈動自如的關節、塑膠材質以及其後的半透明鋼網與金屬絲構圖,經由時間一次次的印證,他找到可資依憑的解決方案。現在,在測試過瓷料、竹子、木頭、紙張與線繩後,他尋找新的方法將這些日常物件界定的藩籬打破。這些材質的催化效果是幾乎無法預期的,在衝擊出現的當下,令貝特必須去重新調整他創作裡詩性語言的配方。萌生出來的是如有機、擁有自我生命般的飄盪不定,而非可預期的幾何式結構。這擁有如草稿般的潛力,上頭打著小結與圈環的線繩有著長長伸出的末端,彷彿能直驅破入時空。線條的細度與瓷料的脆弱度相互對應,就如同残骸與片羽也屬於偉大創作的部分。這極為迷人又脆弱的構造,在物理與視覺上造成必須小心呵護輕盈易碎的印象。在胸針或別針的格式在圖稿與雕塑跳躍轉換,並非像是紀念碑般龐大沉重。而它們所保持的纖細雅緻與坦率直白,也正是力量所在。

Sabine Runde

物件,厚描圖紙,環氧樹脂,低碳鋼絲
Object, transparent paper, epoxy, mild steel wire
Objekt, Transparentpapier, Epoxidharz, Eisendraht
2017, 10 x 7 x 2 cm

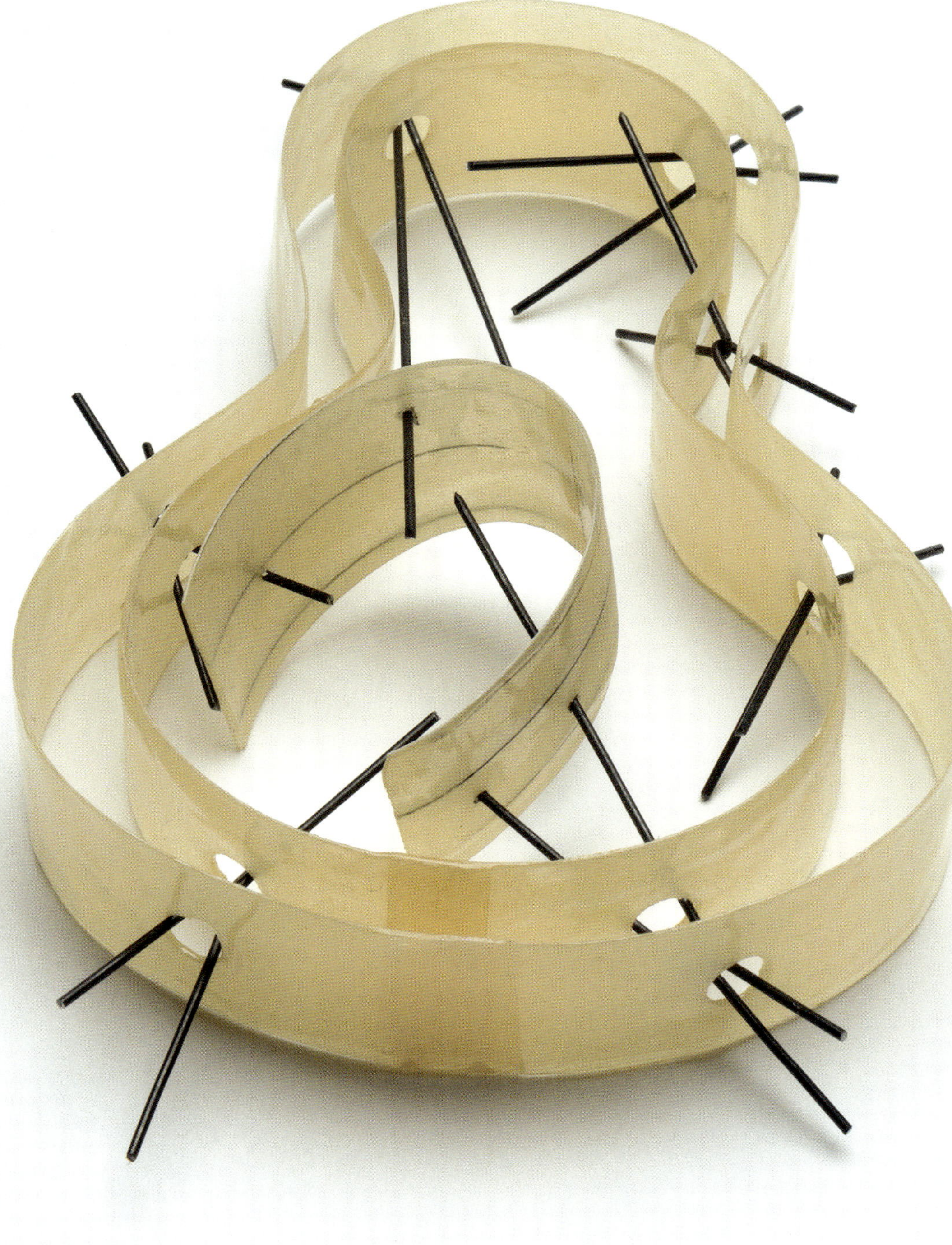

Conclusion

Franz Bette threw himself into this exhibition project with empathy and playful enthusiasm; full of excitement for new experiences, he began a new, open-ended process. From the beginning he could not let go of the idea of overcoming the technoid hardness of metal, especially steel, to convert it into lightness. With his flexible connection, his plastic and later wire compositions with semi-transparent mesh, he found convincing answers to this challenge time and time again. Now in examining porcelain, bamboo, wood, paper and cord, he searches for ways to shift the boundaries further towards the dissolution of everything definite. Their catalytic effect was hardly predictable. Many new impulses have led Franz Bette to special formulations of his poetic language. What has occurred is organic fleetingness instead of the expected geometric constructions. With the potential of a drawing, the cord with its loops and small knots and its long protruding ends can continue into open space. The thinness of the line finds its counterpart in the fragility of the porcelain. Like broken pieces or fragments, these pieces seem to be part of a greater whole. These fragile compositions of great allure, physical and optical lightness evoke care in the handling. In the usual format of brooches and pins, they shift between drawing and sculpture, far removed from all monumentality. Their restrained delicacy and frankness is their strength.

Sabine Runde

物件，厚描圖紙，顏料，低碳鋼絲
Object, transparent paper, paint, mild steel wire
Objekt, Transparentpapier, Farbe, Eisendraht
2017, 8 x 6 x 1.5 cm

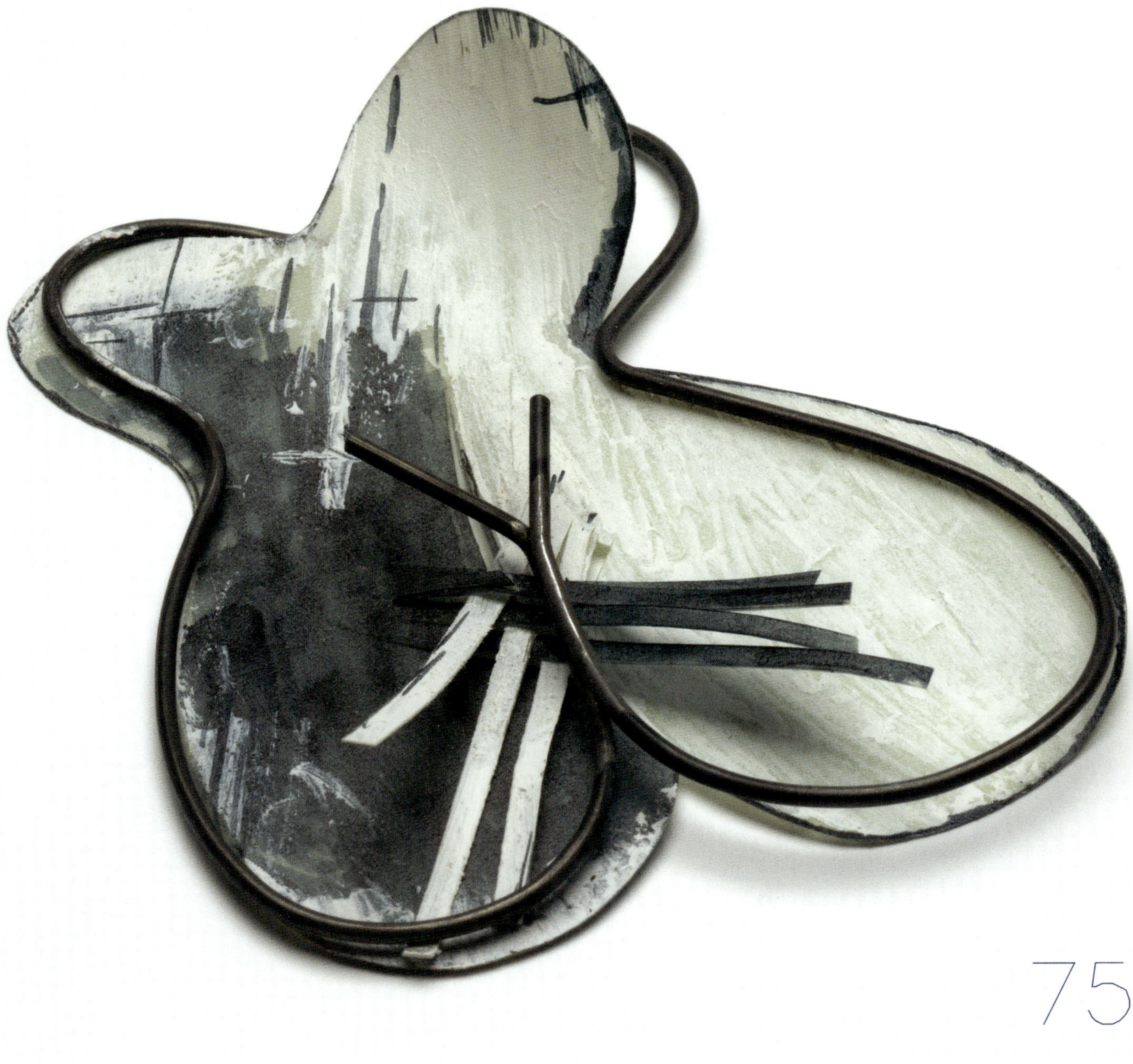

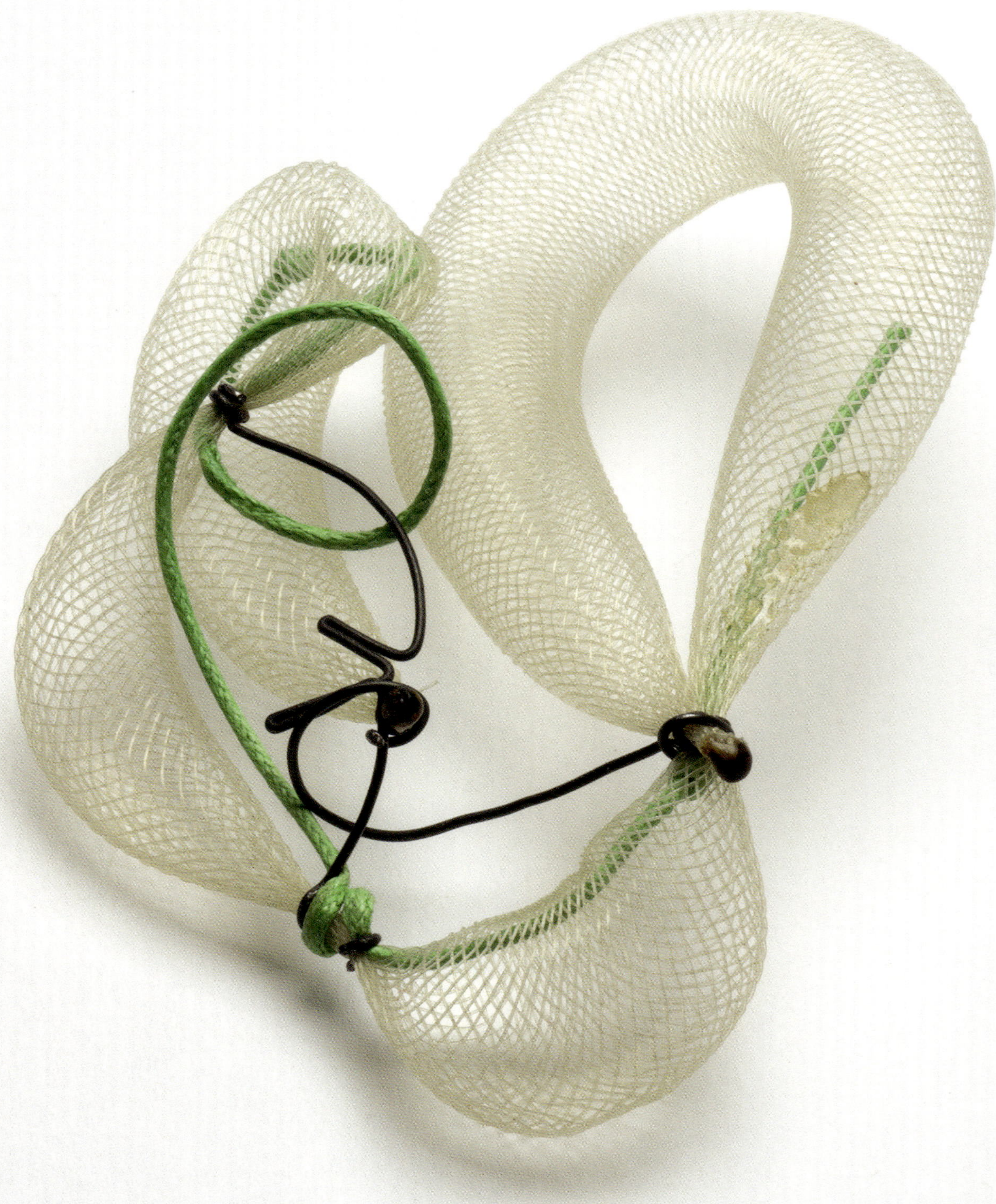

Fazit

Mit Empathie und einem spielerischen Übermut hat sich Franz Bette in dieses Ausstellungsprojekt gestürzt und voller Spannung auf neue Erfahrungen einen Prozess mit offenem Ausgang eingeleitet. Von Anfang an ließ ihn die Idee nicht los, wie Metall im *Schmuck* und gerade die technoide Härte von Stahl überwunden und in Leichtigkeit verwandelt werden könnte. Mit seinen flexiblen Verbindungen, seinen Kunststoff- und späteren Drahtkompositionen mit semitransparenten Metallsieben hat er auf diese Herausforderung immer wieder sehr überzeugende Antworten gefunden. Weitere Grenzverschiebungen in Richtung einer Auflösung alles Definitiven suchte er jetzt in der Auseinandersetzung mit Porzellan, Bambus, Holz, Papier und mit der Schnur. Deren katalytische Wirkung war kaum vorhersehbar. Viele neue Impulse haben Franz Bette zu besonderen Formulierungen in seiner poetischen Sprache geführt. Organische Flüchtigkeit anstelle von erwartungsgemäßer geometrischer Konstruktion hat sich eingestellt. Das Potenzial der Zeichnung kann die Schnur in ihren Schlaufen und kleinen Knoten durch ihre lang auslaufenden Enden weiter in den offenen Raum tragen. Das Filigran der Linie findet eine Entsprechung in der Zerbrechlichkeit des Porzellans. Wie Bruchstücke oder Fragmente scheinen diese Elemente einem größeren Ganzen anzugehören. Diese fragilen Kompositionen von großer Anmut, physischer und optischer Leichtigkeit evozieren Behutsamkeit im Umgang. Im üblichen Format des Ansteckschmucks bewegen sie sich zwischen Zeichnung und Skulptur fern aller Monumentalität. Ihre zurückgenommene Zartheit und Offenheit sind ihre Stärken.

Sabine Runde

物件，塑料網，低碳鋼絲，線繩
Object, plastic mesh, mild steel wire, cord
Objekt, Kunststoffnetz, Eisendraht, Schnur
2012, 6 x 8 x 2 cm

物件,木,顏料,低碳鋼絲

78

物件,木,顏料,低碳鋼絲

Object, wood, paint, mild steel wire

Objekt, Holz, Farbe, Eisendraht

2017, 8 x 8 x 2 cm

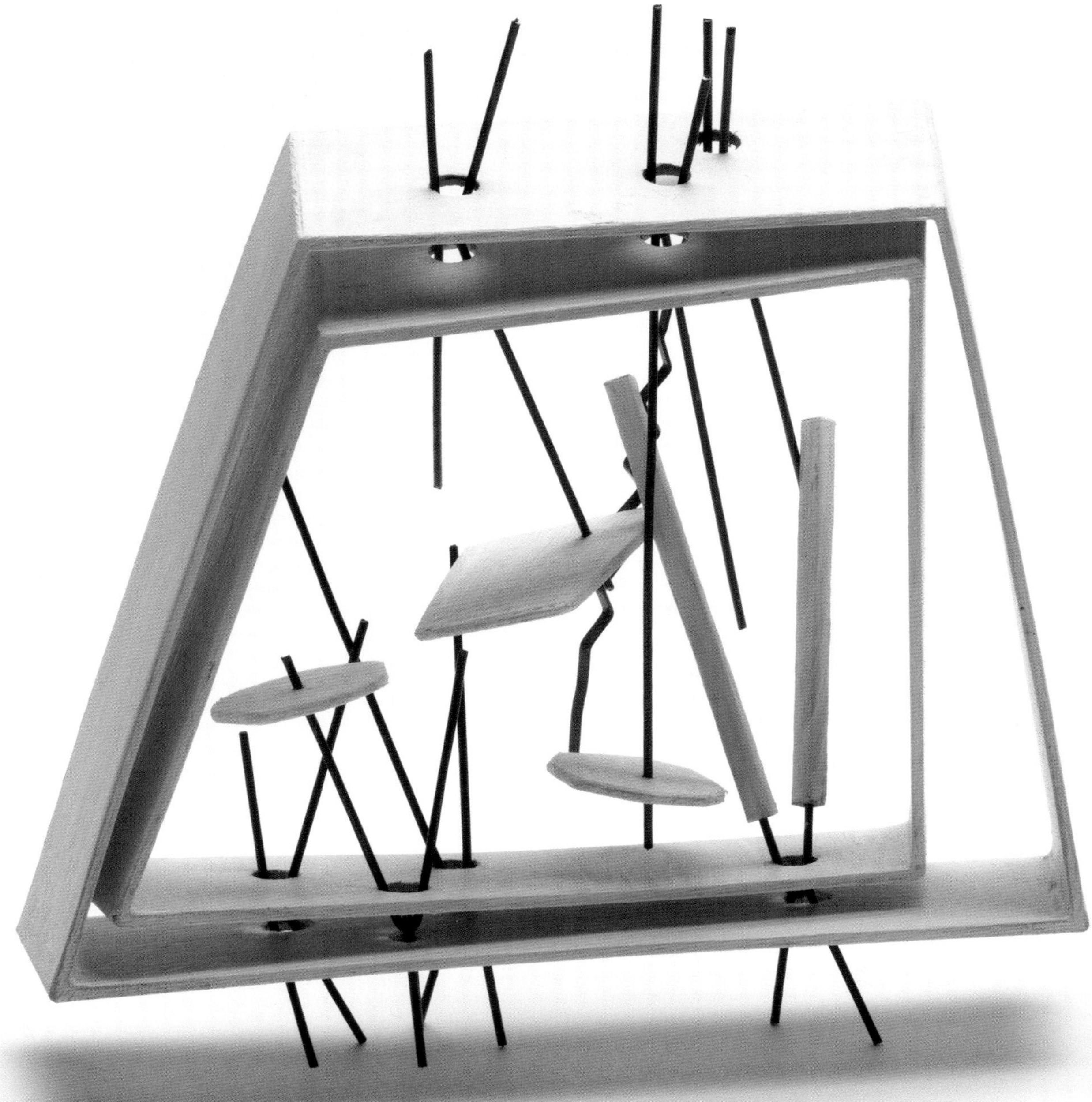

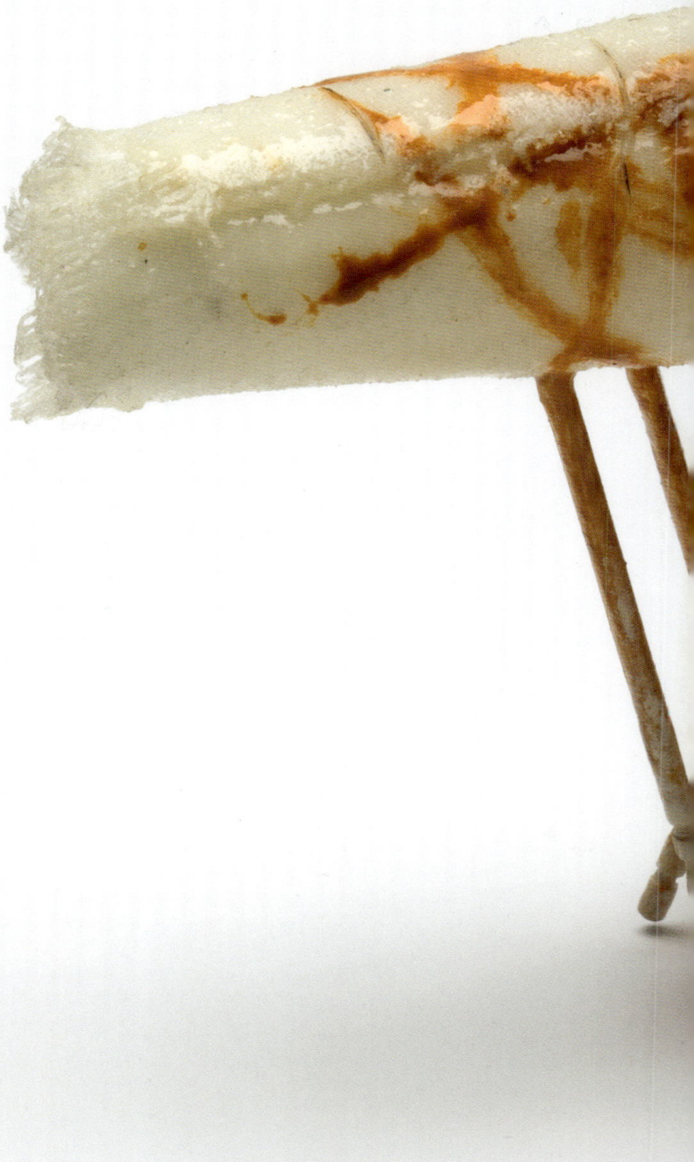

80

物件，亞麻布，環氧樹脂，木
Object, linen, epoxy, wood
Objekt, Leinen, Epoxidharz, Holz
2016, 18 x 10 x 5 cm

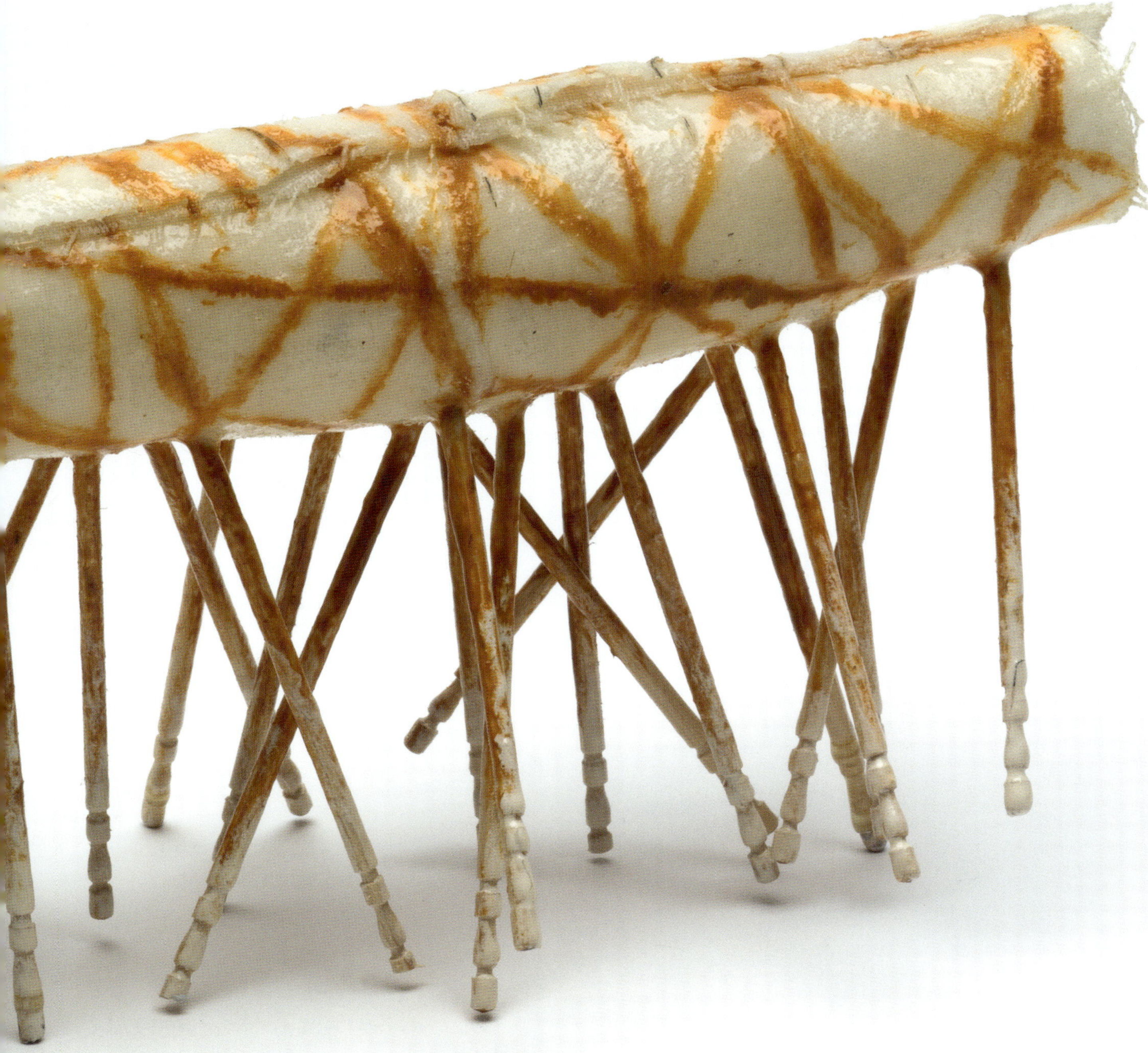

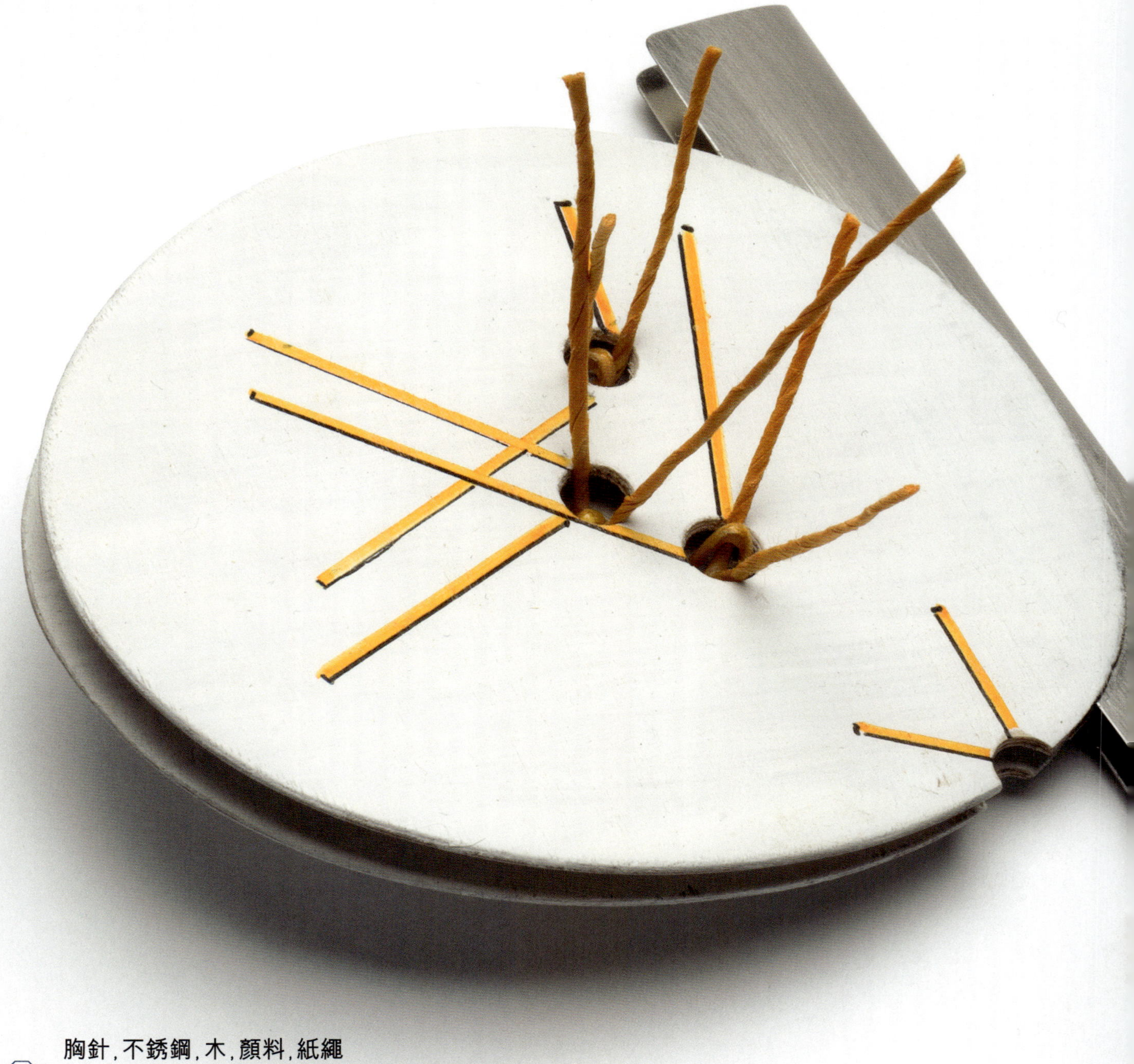

82

胸針,不銹鋼,木,顏料,紙繩
Brooch, stainless steel, wood, paint, paper cord
Brosche, Edelstahl, Holz, Farbe, Papierschnur
2017, 11 x 8 x 5 cm

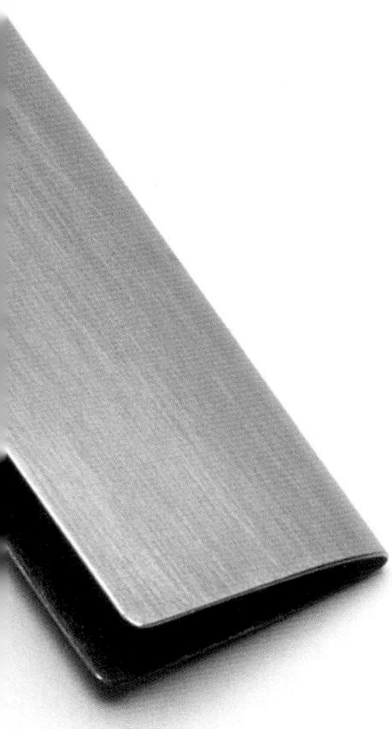

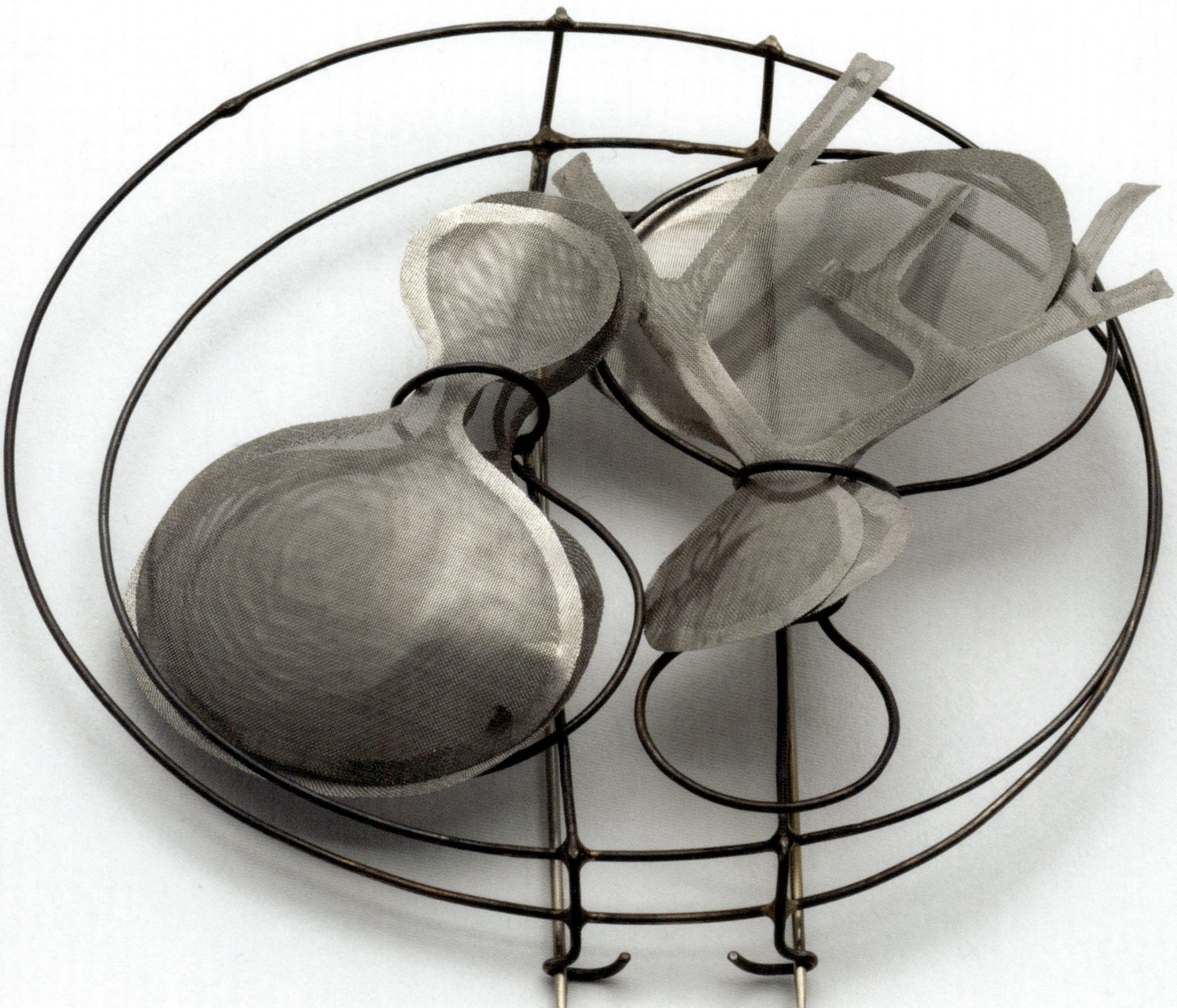

84 胸針，不銹鋼線材，不銹鋼網
Brooch, stainless steel wire, stainless steel mesh
Brosche, Edelstahldraht, Edelstahlnetz
2007, 8 x 8 x 1.5 cm

資歷

Franz Joseph Bette

1941 出生於德國博特羅普

1960-63 向 Friedrich Becker 學習金工碩士課程，杜塞道夫，德國

1963-66 於 Meinrad Burch-Korrodi 擔任金工師及設計師，蘇黎世，瑞士

1967-70 國立設計中心貴金屬部門主任，基爾肯尼，愛爾蘭

1970-73 於寶齊萊珠寶鐘錶公司擔任設計師，琉森，瑞士

1973-94 成立個人設計工作室及工作營，杜塞道夫，德國

1973-75 於歐米茄鐘錶公司擔任設計師，日內瓦，瑞士

1976-85 應用技術大學(FH)講師，杜塞道夫，德國

1985-2006 哈瑙金工學院首飾與器皿大師班首席指導，哈瑙，德國

1989+1990 「高階珠寶設計」研討會主席(歐盟貿易發展計畫)，曼谷，泰國

1992 墨爾本皇家理工大學及國立澳洲大學藝術學院工作營(歌德學院)，澳洲

1997-2001 奧芬巴赫設計學院(HFG)進修及取得文憑，奧芬巴赫，德國

2005 「設計論壇」演講及工作坊，香港，中國

2008-2009 香港知專設計學院講師，香港，中國

2011-2014 香港知專設計學院講師，香港，中國

2012 金澤工藝社「新浪潮金屬論壇」講師，上海，中國

2014 國立台灣工藝研究發展中心「研習工作坊」講師，鶯歌，台灣

2015, 16, 17 玉溪有容教育基金會 Studio 94「十日工作坊」講師，台北，台灣

2017 台南藝術大學「藝術家工作營」講師，台南，台灣

金匠學會成員，國內及國際競賽評審

獎項

1968 戴比爾斯國際鑽飾設計大獎，紐約，美國

1971 瑞士日內瓦市獎盃，日內瓦，瑞士

1974 Dugena 珠寶及設計競賽兩次首獎，佛茨海姆，德國

戴比爾斯今日鑽石獎-男戒，紐約，美國

1983 國際白金大賽銀獎，巴塞爾，瑞士

1983 北萊茵-西發利亞國家獎，杜塞道夫，德國

1986 Gertrud Eysoldt Ring 金環大獎得獎戒指設計首獎，本斯海姆，德國

個展

1977-1990 每年皆於工作室舉辦年度展覽，杜塞道夫，德國

1980 凱悅飯店，達拉斯，美國

Städtische Kellergalerie 藝廊，杜塞道夫，德國

1981 凱悅飯店，休士頓，美國

1982 VEBA House，杜塞道夫，德國

1988 德國金工之家，哈瑙，德國

1990 科堡藝術協會，科堡，德國

2003 首飾之家，施里斯海姆，德國

2007 應用藝術博物館，法蘭克福，德國

2008 Maurer Zilioli藝廊，慕尼黑，德國

2014 國立臺灣博物館南門園區，國立台灣工藝研究發展中心，台北，台灣

精選聯展 (2004 年後)

2004 「Ausgepackt/Unpacked」, 德國金工之家, 哈瑙, 德國
2008 「極致首飾」, Maurer Zilioli 當代藝術, 慕尼黑, 德國
2009 「枕上首飾」, Kunstbüro Reillplast藝廊, Maurer Zilioli 當代藝術, 慕尼黑, 德國
2010 「盒子」, Kunstbüro Reillplast 藝廊, Maurer Zilioli當代藝術, 慕尼黑, 德國
2012 「新北市2012德國當代金工大展」, 黃金博物館, 新北市, 台灣
「十年·有聲 - 當代國際首飾展」, 中央美術學院美術館, 北京, 中國
2015 「石間-國際當代首飾展」, Sabato Lab·飾研所, 台北, 台灣
2016 「秘密自白」, CODA博物館, 阿珀爾多倫, 荷蘭
2017 「秘密自白」, 斯托克別墅, 慕尼黑, 德國
「粉紅色呈現之美-首飾的灰色顯性」, 佛茨海姆首飾博物館, 佛茨海姆, 德國

典藏

德國科隆, Von Lom 私人收藏
德國法蘭克福, 應用藝術博物館
德國漢堡, Amme 私人收藏
德國漢堡, 德國金工之家
台灣高雄, 永添藝術·金馬賓館
德國佛茨海姆, 首飾博物館
德國伍珀塔爾, Abeler 私人收藏
瑞士蘇黎世, 蘇黎世國家博物館, Alice and Louis Koch Collection

眾多私人收藏

文獻

2003 年前出版品請參閱2007年德國法蘭克福Sabine Runde博士之著作「Ornament without Ornament, Franz Bette Jewellery」/ till 2003 see Sabine Runde, Ornament without Ornament, Franz Bette Jewellery, Frankfurt am Main 2007 (ISBN 978-3-88270-112 8)

2003 Arch Gregory, Minimal Rings, n.p. 2003, pp. 15, 18, 41, 43 (ISBN 0-9747573-0-1)
2007 Jochen Amme, Historische Bestecke 2, Stuttgart 2007, pp. 180, 203, 207 (ISBN 978-3-89790-261-9)
2012 Fei Teng (ed.), 10 Years – Re: Jewellery, Beijing 2012, pp. 188-191 (ISBN 978-7-5064-9322-2); Cornelie Holzach, Wang-Mong Raun, German Contemporary Metal Crafts, New Taipei City 2012, pp. 67-8 (ISBN 978-986-03-2768-7)
2014 Pamela Auburn, Same but Different, Nan-Tou 2014 (ISBN 978-986-04-1067-9)
2016 Ellen Maurer-Zilioli, Private Confessions, Stuttgart 2016, pp. 25, 35, 150-53 (ISBN 978-3-89790-476-7)
2017 Julia Kleinbeck, Katja Poljanac, Andreas Volz, Pretty on Pink – graue Eminenzen des Schmucks, Schmuckmuseum Pforzheim, Pforzheim 2017, pp. 18-19, 26 (ISBN 978-3-933924-23-0); Daniela Malev, To the Point, Leipzig 2017, pp. 220-1, 241 (ISBN 978-3-96014-390-1)

1985 至 2014年間出版眾多學生作品圖錄及期刊發表

戒指, 不鏽鋼, 不銹鋼網
Ring, stainless steel, stainless steel mesh
Ring, Edelstahl, Edelstahlnetz
2002, 3 x 5 x 2.5 cm

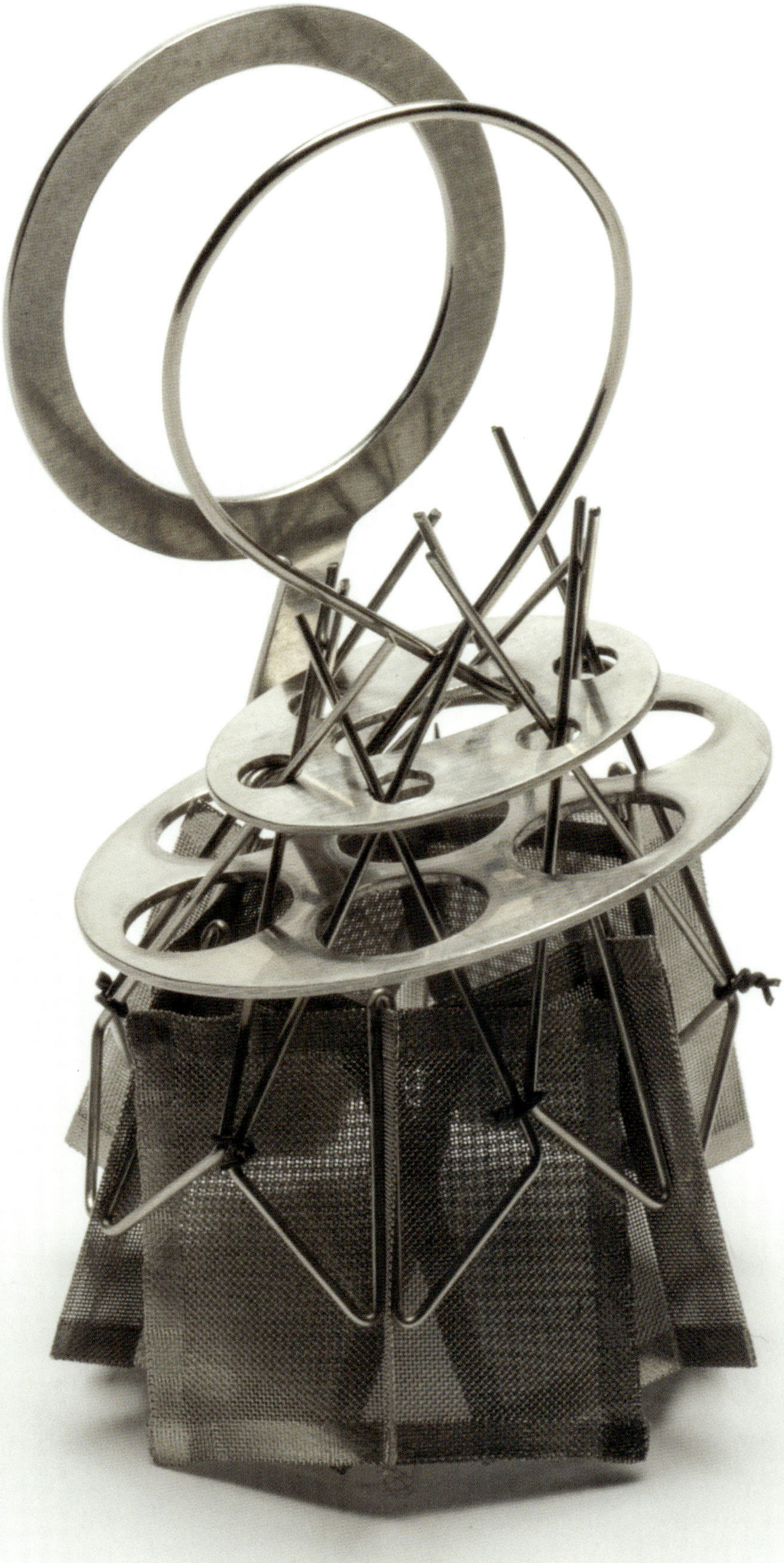

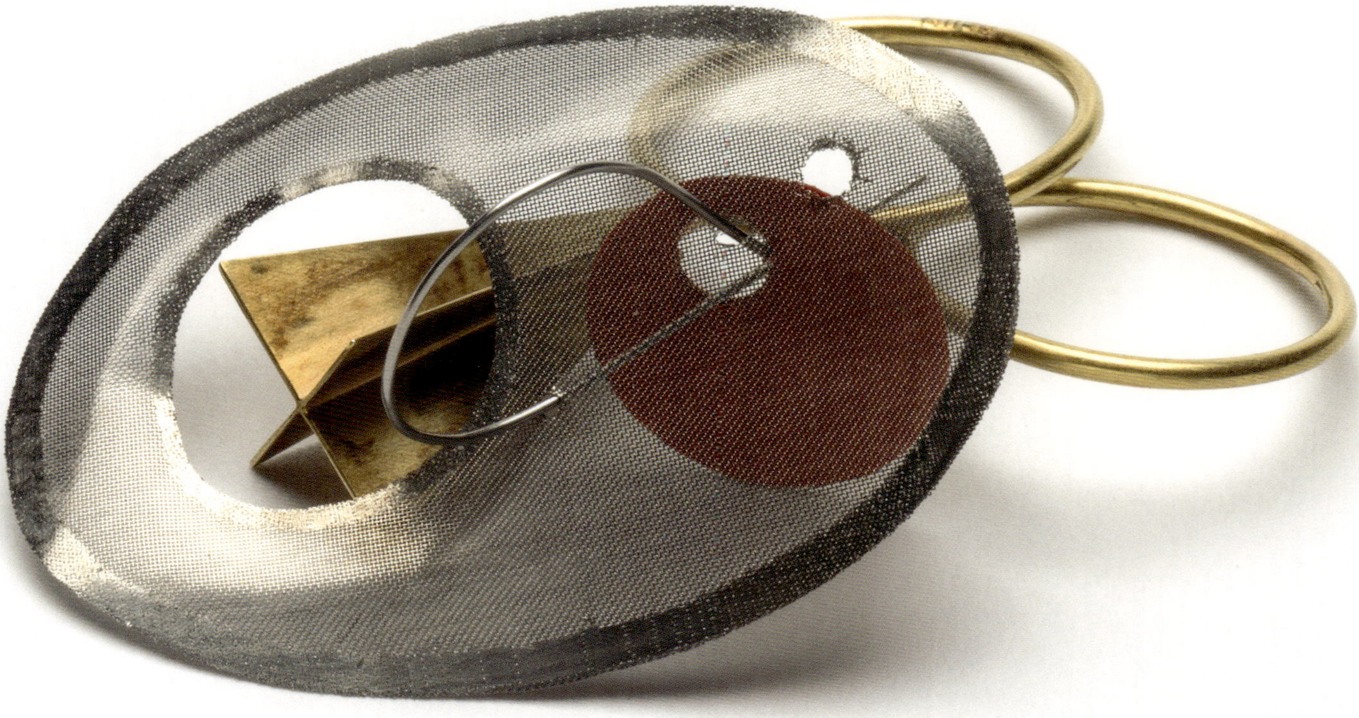

88 戒指，金，不銹鋼，顏料
Ring, gold, stainless steel, paint
Ring, Gold, Edelstahl, Farbe
2006, 4.5 x 4 x 3 cm

Curriculum Vitae

Franz Joseph Bette

1941	Born in Bottrop, Germany
1960-63	Düsseldorf, Germany, gold and silversmith education with Professor Friedrich Becker — master student
1963-66	Zurich, Switzerland, goldsmith & designer, Meinrad Burch-Korrodi
1967-70	Kilkenny, Ireland, National Design Centre, head of Precious Metal Department
1970-73	Lucerne, Switzerland, designer, Bucherer
1973-94	Düsseldorf, Germany, established own design studios and workshop
1973-75	Geneva, Switzerland, designer, Omega
1976-85	Düsseldorf, Germany, Fachhochschule (advanced technical college) lecturer
1985-2006	Hanau, Germany, Staatliche Zeichenakademie, leader of Master Class for Jewellery and Holloware
1989, 1990	Bangkok, Thailand, "Advanced Jewellery Design", seminar leader (European Union Trade Development Programme)
1992	Melbourne, Australia, RMIT University and Canberra, Australia, ANU, School of Art, workshops (Goethe Institute)
1997-2001	Offenbach, Germany, Hochschule für Gestaltung (HfG), studies and diploma
2005	Hong Kong, China, "Design Symposium": presentation and workshop
2008-2009	Hong Kong, China, Design Institute, lecturer
2011-2014	Hong Kong, China, Design Institute, lecturer
2012	Jin Ze Arts Centre, Shanghai, China, New Wave Metal Symposium, lecture
2014	Yingge, Taiwan, National Taiwan Craft Research and Development Institute (NTCRI), workshop
2015,16,17	Taipei, Taiwan, Thermos Foundation, Studio 94, workshops
2017	Tainan, Taiwan, Tainan National University of the Arts, workshop

Member of the Gesellschaft für Goldschmiedekunst (Goldsmith's Society); Juror for national and international competitions

Awards

1968	New York, USA, De Beers Diamond International Award
1971	Geneva, Switzerland, Trophy of the City of Geneva
1974	Pforzheim, Germany, Dugena Jewellery and Design Competition, two 1st prizes New York, USA, De Beers Diamonds Today — Men's Ring
1983	Basel, Switzerland, International Platinum Competition, 2nd prize
1983	Düsseldorf, Germany, State Prize of Nordrhein-Westfalen
1986	Bensheim, Germany, Gertrud Eysoldt Ring, 1st prize

Solo Exhibitions

1977–1999	Düsseldorf, Germany, annual exhibitions in own studio
1980	Dallas, USA, Hyatt Regency Düsseldorf, Germany, Städtische Kellergalerie
1981	Houston, USA, Hyatt Regency
1982	Düsseldorf, Germany, VEBA House
1988	Hanau, Germany, Deutsches Goldschmiedehaus
1990	Coburg, Germany, Kunstverein
2003	Schriesheim, Germany, Schmuck Haus
2007	Frankfurt am Main, Germany, Museum of Applied Art
2008	Munich, Germany, Maurer Zilioli
2014	Taipei, Taiwan, National Taiwan Museum Nanmen Park, NTCRI

Selected group exhibitions, since 2004

2004 Hanau, Germany, Deutsches Goldschmiedehaus, Ausgepackt/Unpacked,

2008 Munich, Germany, Maurer Zilioli Contemporary Arts, Schmuck Extreme

2009 Munich, Germany, Kunstbüro Reillplast, Maurer Zilioli Contemporary Arts, Pillow Jewellery

2010 Munich, Germany, Kunstbüro Reillplast, Maurer Zilioli Comtemporary Arts, The Box

2012 New Taipei City, Taiwan, Gold Museum, German Contemporary Metal Crafts
Beijing, China, cafa Art Museum, 10 Years – Re: Jewellery

2015 Taipei, Taiwan, Sabato Lab, Cabinet de Curiosités

2016 Apeldoorn, Netherlands, CODA Museum, Private Confessions

2017 Munich, Germany, Villa Stuck, Private Confessions
Pforzheim, Germany, Schmuckmuseum, Pretty on Pink – graue Eminenzen des Schmucks (Grey Eminences of Jewellery)

Collections

Cologne, Germany, Von Lom Collection
Frankfurt am Main, Germany, Museum Angewandte Kunst
Hamburg, Germany, Amme Collection
Hanau, Germany, Deutsches Goldschmiedehaus
Kaohsiung, Taiwan, ALIEN Art Centre
Pforzheim, Germany, Schmuckmuseum
Wuppertal, Germany, Abeler Collection
Zurich, Switzerland, Swiss National Museum, Alice and Louis Koch Collection
Numerous private collections

Literature

until 2003 see Sabine Runde, Ornament without Ornament, Franz Bette Jewellery, Frankfurt am Main 2007 (ISBN 978-3-88270-112-8)

2003 Arch Gregory, Minimal Rings, n.p. 2003, pp. 15, 18, 41, 43 (ISBN 0-9747673-0-1)

2007 Jochen Amme, Historische Bestecke II, Stuttgart 2007, pp. 180, 203, 207 (ISBN 978-3-89790-261-9)

2012 Fei Teng (ed.), 10 Years - Re: Jewellery, CAFA Art Museum, Beijing 2012, pp. 188-191 (ISBN 978-7-5064-9322-2)
Cornelie Holzach, Wang-Mong Raun, German Contemporary Metal Crafts, New Taipei City 2012, pp. 67-8 (ISBN 978-986-03-2768-7)

2014 Pamela Auburn, Same but Different, Nan-Tou 2014 (ISBN 978-986-04-1067-9)

2016 Ellen Maurer-Zilioli, Private Confessions, Stuttgart 2016, pp. 25, 35, 150-53 (ISBN 978-3-89790-476-7)

2017 Julia Kleinbeck, Katja Poljanac, Andreas Volz, Pretty on Pink – graue Eminenzen des Schmucks, Schmuckmuseum Pforzheim, Pforzheim 2017, pp. 18-19, 26 (ISBN 978-3-933924-23-0);
Daniela Malev, To the Point, Leipzig 2017, pp. 220-1, 241 (ISBN 978-3-96014-390-1)

From 1985 to 2014 numerous catalogues of student work and journals

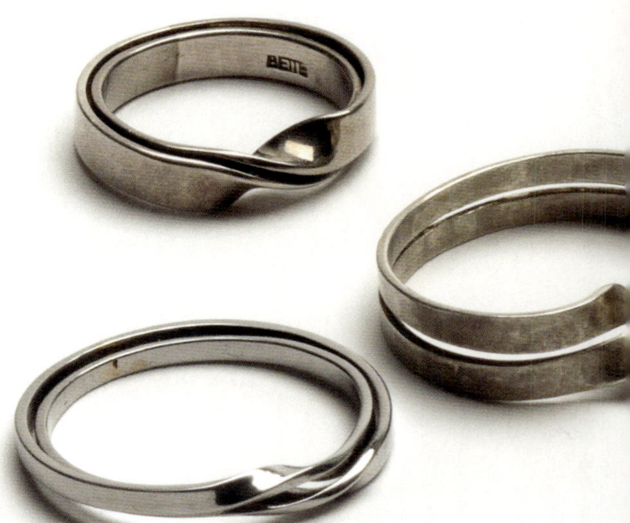

戒指系列,銀,鈀金,鎢
Ring series, silver, palladium, tungsten
Ring Serie, Silber, Palladium, Wolfram
2012, 2 x 2 cm

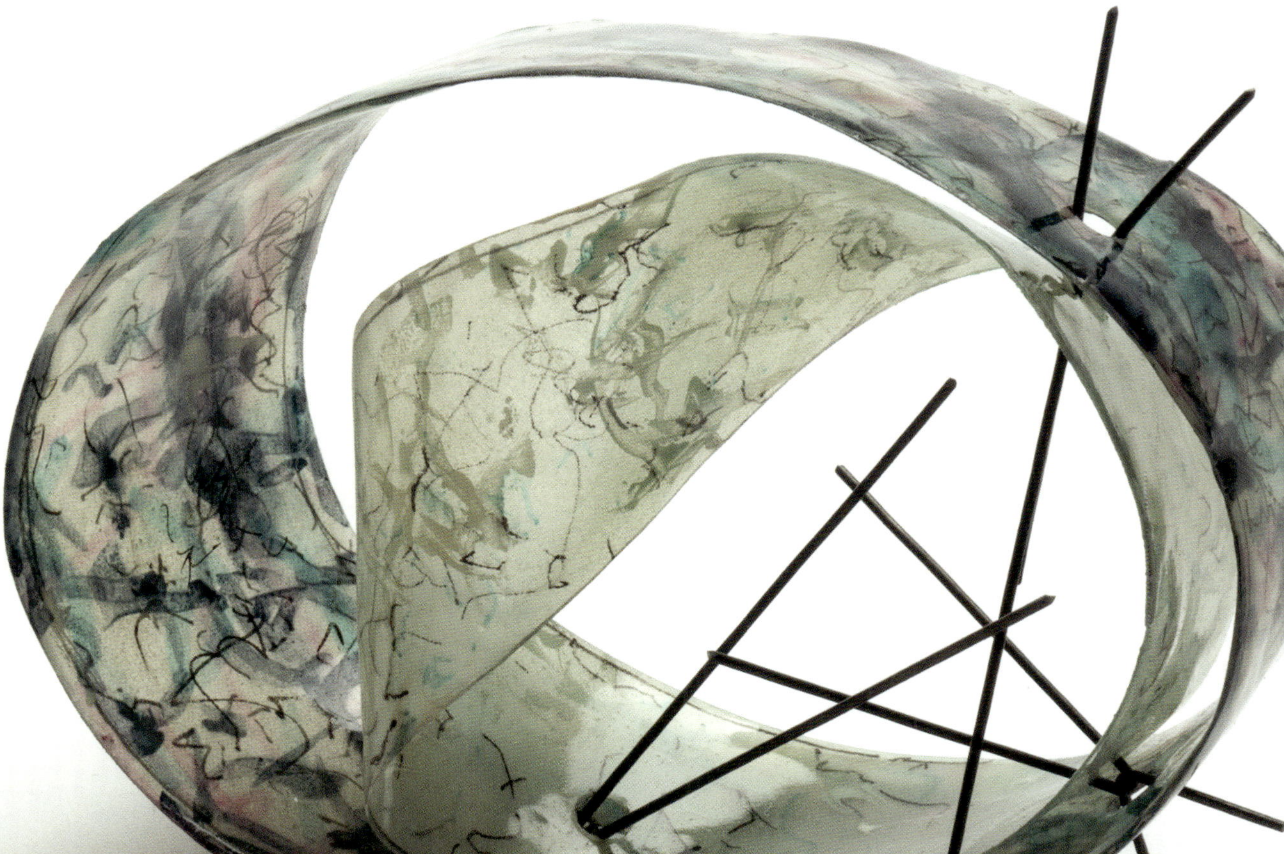

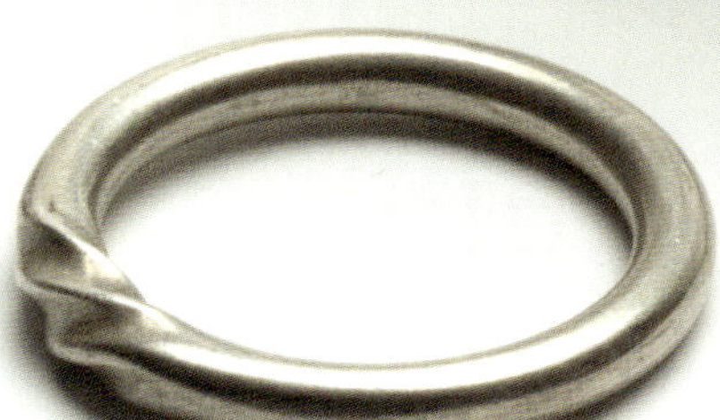

物件，紙材，環氧樹脂，低碳鋼絲
Object, paper, epoxy, mild steel wire
Objekt, Papier, Epoxidharz, Eisendraht
2017, 9 x 8 x 3.5 cm

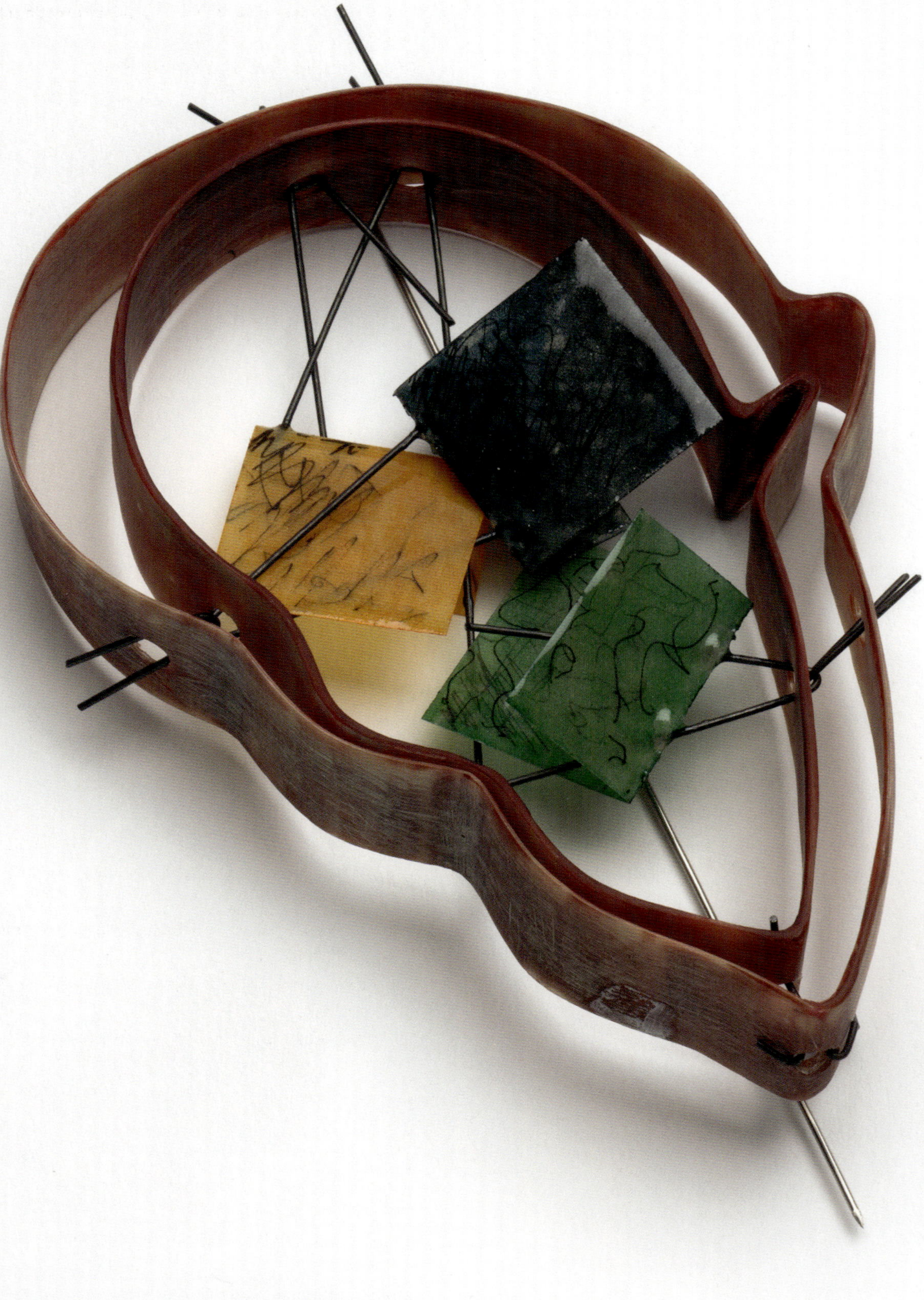

92 胸針,紙材,環氧樹脂,低碳鋼絲
Brooch, paper, epoxy, mild steel wire
Brosche, Papier, Epoxidharz, Eisendraht
2017, 12 x 8 x 3 cm

Vita

Franz Joseph Bette

1941	geboren in Bottrop
1960–63	Düsseldorf, Gold- und Silberschmiedeausbildung bei Professor Friedrich Becker, Meisterschüler
1963–66	Zürich, Schweiz, Meinrad Burch-Korrodi
1967–70	Kilkenny, Irland, National Design Centre (NDC), Leiter der Designabteilung Edelmetall
1970–73	Luzern, Schweiz, Bucherer, Designer
1973–94	Düsseldorf, eigenes Atelier
1973–75	Genf, Schweiz, Omega, Designer
1976–85	Düsseldorf, Fachhochschule, Lehrtätigkeit
1985–2006	Hanau, Staatliche Zeichenakademie, Leiter der Meisterklasse für Schmuck und Gerät
1989 + 1990	Bangkok, Thailand, „Advanced Jewellery Design“, Seminarleitung (Wirtschaftsförderung der Europäischen Union)
1992	Melbourne, Australien, RMIT Universität, und Canberra, Australien, Canberra School of Art, Workshops (Goethe-Institut)
1997–2001	Offenbach, Hochschule für Gestaltung, Studium, Diplom
2005	Hongkong, China, Design Symposium, Präsentation und Workshop
2008–2009	Hongkong, China, Design Institute, Lehrtätigkeit
2011–2014	Hongkong, China, Design Institute, Lehrtätigkeit
2012	Jin Ze Arts Centre, China, Symposium, New Wave Metal Symposium, Vortrag
2014	Yingge, Taiwan, National Taiwan Craft Research and Development Institute (NTCRI), Workshop
2015,16,17	Taipeh, Taiwan, Thermosstiftung – Studio 94, Workshops
2017	Tainan, Taiwan, Tainan National University of the Arts, Workshop

Mitglied der Gesellschaft für Goldschmiedekunst; Juror bei nationalen und internationalen Wettbewerben.

Auszeichnungen

1968	New York, USA, De Beers Diamond International Award
1971	Genf, Schweiz, Preis der Stadt Genf
1974	Pforzheim, Dugena Schmuck und Design Wettbewerb, zwei erste Preise New York, USA, De Beers Diamonds Today – Herren-Ring
1983	Basel, Schweiz, Internationaler Platin Wettbewerb, 2. Preis
1983	Düsseldorf, Staatspreis des Landes Nordrhein-Westfalen
1986	Bensheim, Gertrud-Eysoldt-Ring, 1. Preis

Einzelausstellungen

1977–1990	Düsseldorf, Jahresausstellungen im eigenen Atelier
1980	Dallas, USA, Hyatt Regency Düsseldorf, Städtische Kellergalerie
1981	Houston, USA, Hyatt Regency
1982	Düsseldorf, VEBA-Haus
1988	Hanau, Deutsches Goldschmiedehaus, Schmuck – Objekte – Bilder
1990	Coburg, Kunstverein Coburg e.V.
2003	Schriesheim, Schmuckhaus
2007	Frankfurt am Main, Museum Angewandte Kunst
2008	München, Galerie Maurer Zilioli Contemporary Arts
2014	Taipeh, Taiwan, National Taiwan Museum – Nanmen Park, NTCRI

Gruppenausstellungen seit 2004

2004	Hanau, Deutsches Goldschmiedehaus, Ausgepackt
2008	München, Galerie Maurer Zilioli Contemporary Arts, Schmuck Extreme
2009	München, Kunstbüro Reillplast, Galerie Maurer Zilioli Contemporary Arts, Pillow Jewellery
2010	München, Kunstbüro Reillplast, Galerie Maurer Zilioli Contemporary Arts, The Box
2012	Neu-Taipeh, Taiwan, Gold Museum, German Contemporary Metal Crafts Beijing, China, CAFA Art Museum, 10 Years – Re: Jewelry
2015	Taipeh, Taiwan, Sabato Lab, Cabinet de Curiosités
2016	Apeldoorn, Niederlande, CODA Museum, Private Confessions
2017	München, Villa Stuck, Private Confessions Pforzheim, Schmuckmuseum, Pretty on Pink – graue Eminenzen des Schmucks

Sammlungen

Frankfurt am Main, Museum Angewandte Kunst
Hanau, Deutsches Goldschmiedehaus
Hamburg, Sammlung Ammer
Kaohsiung, Taiwan, ALIEN Art
Köln, Sammlung Von Lom
Pforzheim, Schmuckmuseum
Wuppertal, Sammlung Abeler
Zürich, Schweiz, Landesmuseum Zürich, Sammlung Alice und Louis Koch
Diverse Privatsammlungen

Literatur

bis 2003 s. Sabine Runde, Franz Bette, Schmuck – Ornament ohne Ornament, Frankfurt am Main 2007 (ISBN 978-3-88270-112-8)

2003 Arch Gregory, Minimal Rings, o. O. 2003, S. 15, 18, 41, 43 (ISBN 0-9747673-0-1)

2007 Jochen Amme, Historische Bestecke II, Stuttgart 2007, S. 180, 203, 207 (ISBN 978-3-89790-261-9)

2012 Fei Teng (Hrsg.), 10 Years – Re: Jewellery, CAFA Art Museum, Beijing 2012, S. 188–191 (ISBN 978-7-5064-9322-2)
Cornelie Holzach, Wang–Mong Raun, German Contemporary Metal Crafts, Gold Museum, New Taipei City 2012, S. 67–8 (ISBN 978-986-03-2768-7

2014 Pamela Auburn, Same but Different, Nan-Tou 2014 (ISNB 978-986-04-1067-9)

2016 Ellen Maurer Zilioli, Private Confessions, CODA Museum, Apeldoorn / Villa Stuck, München, Stuttgart 2016, S. 25, 35, 150–53 (ISBN 978-3-89790-476-7)

2017 Julia Kleinbeck, Katja Poljanac, Andreas Volz, Pretty on Pink – graue Eminenzen des Schmucks, Schmuckmuseum Pforzheim, Pforzheim 2017, S. 18–19, 26 (ISBN 978-3-933924-23-0)
Daniela Malev, To the Point, Borsdorf bei Leipzig 2017, S. 220–1, 241 (ISBN 978-3-96014-390-1)

1985 bis 2014, diverse Studenten und Klassenkataloge sowie Zeitschriften.

94

物件，合板，顏料，紙繩
Object, plywood, paint, paper cord
Objekt, Schichtholz, Farbe, Papierschnur
2018, 5 x 4 x 2 cm

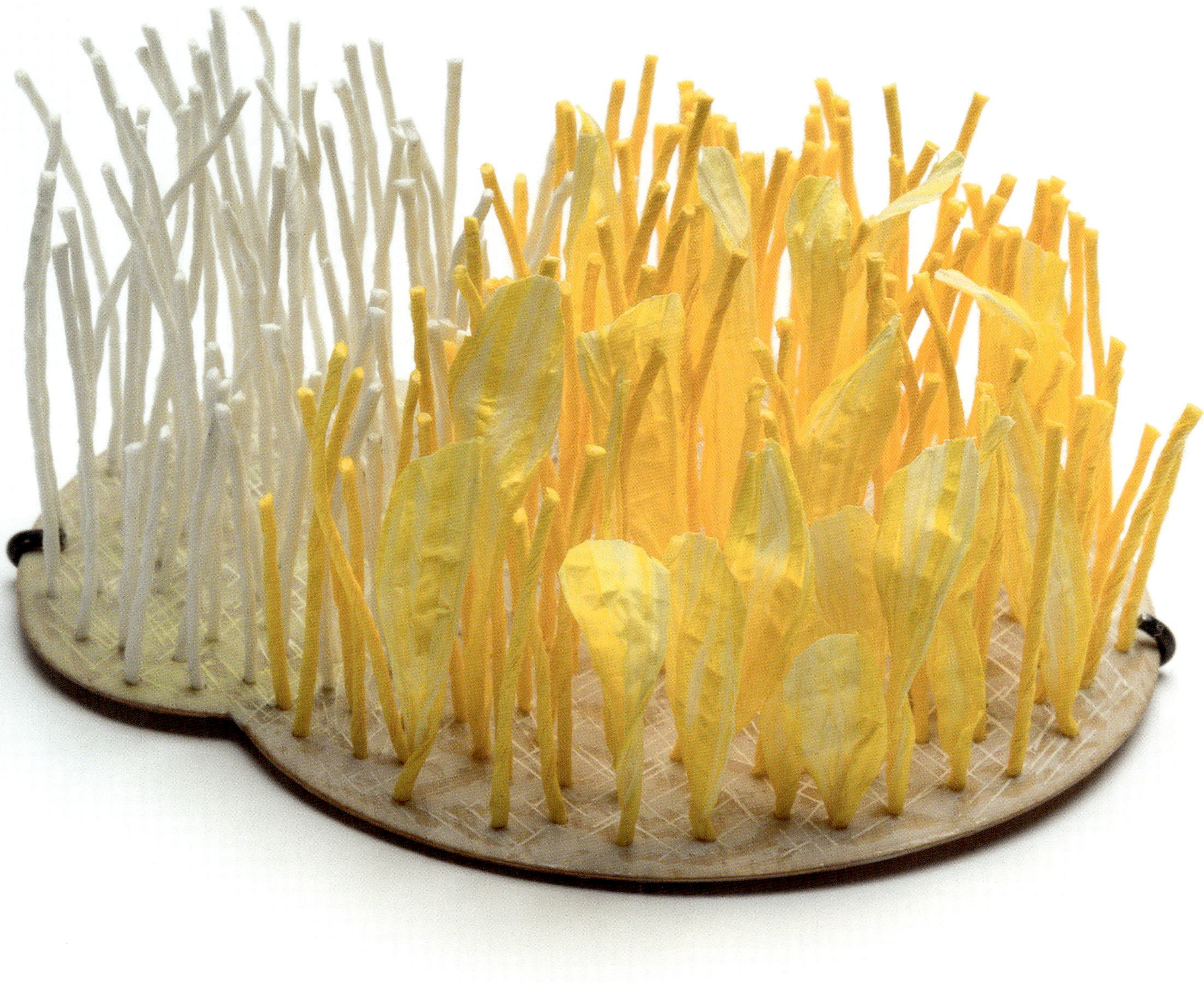

出版說明

編輯 / Editor / Herausgeber:
ALIEN Art 永添藝術, Kaohsiung 高雄, Taiwan 台灣
Museum Angewandte Kunst, Frankfurt am Main, Germany 德國
Franz Bette, Lörrach, Germany 德國

作者 / Authors / Autoren:
Sabine Runde, Museum Angewandte Kunst in Frankfurt am Main, Germany
邵雅曼 Yaman Shao, 執行長 Director, 永添藝術 ALIEN Art, 高雄 Kaohsiung, 台灣 Taiwan

內容與編輯 / Concept and editing / Konzeption und Redaktion:
Franz Bette, Lörrach, Germany 德國
Sabine Runde

永添藝術專案及展覽整合執行 /
Project and exhibition coordinator of ALIEN Art /
Projekt- und Ausstellungskoordination bei ALIEN Art:
Virna Lee 李岱芸, Tainan 台南, Taiwan 台灣

專案整合 / Project coordinator / Projektkoordination
Arnoldsche Art Publishers:
Greta Garle, Stuttgart, Germany 德國

編譯 / Translator / Übersetzung:
Pamela Auburn, Lörrach (德文 / 英文; German / English; Deutsch / Englisch)
王章貞 Tracy Wang, 台南 Tainan, 台灣 Taiwan
(英文 / 中文; English / Chinese; Englisch / Chinesisch)
Sabine Runde / Nora von Achenbach (英文 / 德文; English / German; Englisch / Deutsch)

中文翻譯潤筆 / Chinese Editing and Proofreading / Redaktion in Taiwan:
Zeni Sen 錢亞東, Tainan 台南, Taiwan 台灣

平面設計 / Graphic designer / Grafische Gestaltung:
VIER5, Paris 巴黎, France 法國

印刷 / Printed by / Druck:
GTS, Kranj, Slovenia

用紙 / Paper / Papier:
Luxo Art Samt 170 gsm

攝影及影像編輯 / Image editing and Photo credits / Bildbearbeitung und Bildnachweis:
Wolfgang Günzel, Offenbach, Germany 德國

封面插圖 / Cover illustrations / Umschlagabbildungen:
Wolfgang Günzel, Offenbach, Germany 德國

本書為「紅X線：Franz Bette 首飾」特展發行圖錄 / The present publication is published on the occasion of the exhibition "Red X Thread" /
Die vorliegende Publikation erscheint anlässlich der Ausstellung „Der rote Faden: Franz Bette – Schmuck"

策劃暨展覽設計 / Organization and exhibition design / Organisation und Ausstellungsdesign:
ALIEN Art, Taiwan 永添藝術, 台灣; Museum Angewandte Kunst, Frankfurt am Main; Franz Bette, Lörrach

書目資訊收錄於德國國家圖書館
德國國家圖書館收錄本書於德國國家書目中, 書目資訊可於線上檢索查詢: www.dnb.de /
Bibliographic information published by the Deutsche Nationalbibliothek: The Deutsche Nationalbibliothek lists this publication in the Deutsche Nationalbibliografie; detailed bibliographic data are available on the Internet at www.dnb.de. /
Bibliografische Information der Deutschen Nationalbibliothek: Die Deutsche Nationalbibliothek verzeichnet diese Publikation in der Deutschen Nationalbibliografie; detaillierte bibliografische Daten sind im Internet über www.dnb.de abrufbar.

ISBN 978-3-89790-544-3

印製於歐洲, 2019 / Made in Europe, 2019

ALIEN 永添藝術 ALIEN Art museumangewandtekunst